Terra Ludus

Social Fictions Series

Series Editor
Patricia Leavy
USA

The *Social Fictions* series emerges out of the arts-based research movement. The series includes full-length fiction books that are informed by social research but written in a literary/artistic form (novels, plays, and short story collections). Believing there is much to learn through fiction, the series only includes works written entirely in the literary medium adapted. Each book includes an academic introduction that explains the research and teaching that informs the book as well as how the book can be used in college courses. The books are underscored with social science or other scholarly perspectives and intended to be relevant to the lives of college students—to tap into important issues in the unique ways that artistic or literary forms can.

Please email queries to pleavy7@aol.com

International Editorial Advisory Board

Terra Ludus

A Novel about Media, Gender and Sport

Toni Bruce

SENSE PUBLISHERS
ROTTERDAM/BOSTON/TAIPEI

A C.I.P. record for this book is available from the Library of Congress.

ISBN: 978-94-6300-768-9 (paperback)
ISBN: 978-94-6300-769-6 (hardback)
ISBN: 978-94-6300-770-2 (e-book)

Published by: Sense Publishers,
P.O. Box 21858,
3001 AW Rotterdam,
The Netherlands
https://www.sensepublishers.com/

All chapters in this book have undergone peer review.

Printed on acid-free paper

PRAISE FOR
TERRA LUDUS

"Surely a new classic, *Terra Ludus* reverberates in the traditions of both Aotearoa literature and best basketball fiction. Toni Bruce reassembles sport into a narrative imbued with high fashion, futurology, beloved characters, and collective tales of patriarchy-womanhood-sensuality. Bruce vividly – I laughed, cried, appreciated irony, quickly read ahead – narrates a future world that she and her characters interlace with fresh and sometimes shocking sport-media tropes and turns of plot. For Bruce, the future of sport is both terrifying and wondrous and for those reasons alone, I loved this book – it's smart and never typical – beach reading and graduate seminar material all at once."
– Synthia Sydnor, Ph.D., University of Illinois at Urbana-Champaign

"*Terra Ludus* is entertaining fiction that actually gets us thinking about the complicated and often disturbing relations of the commercialism of sports, the globalism of media and the persistence of gender bias and violence. Using popular culture pedagogically to think about popular culture and power, *Terra Ludus* is a valuable tool for critical thought."
– Lawrence Grossberg, Ph.D., University of North Carolina at Chapel Hill

"Imaginatively grounded in patriarchal and misogynist worldviews, *Terra Ludus* describes a future world where unbalanced opportunities for sportspeople remain. It is both engaging and thoughtful, a balance between a literary, thought-provoking and exciting story. We follow Daniela Bartoli, a feminist social justice warrior who fights for equity and opportunity for women in a dystopian future where sport opportunities for skilled female basketball players *still* are limited. She becomes the face of a new league, suffering misogynist threats and soldiering on for equal opportunity. Toni Bruce has produced a *tour de force*. She confronts the dominance of male sport in popular culture,

media and popular consciousness by writing a future world, not unlike our own, where sexism is still very real. *Terra Ludus* makes us ponder whether each new generation has to fight for social justice anew."
– Robert Rinehart, Ph.D., University of Waikato

"*Terra Ludus* is a *sine qua non* tale about Third Wave Feminism. Set in a future society, it asks: What could happen if dominant ideas about women, sports, sexuality, ethnicity and the media left over from the Twentieth-Century are challenged head-on by women athletes? Finding out will keep readers reading, students buzzing."
– Laurel Richardson, Ph.D., The Ohio State University

"Toni Bruce, sports reporter, sport columnist and academic, turns her keen literary eye on the spectacular failure of sport studies scholars and activists to convince mainstream sports media to increase coverage of women's sport. Her gripping story turns this narrative on its head, and shows all of us how things could be different. *Terra Ludus* is a story about what can happen when long-held ideas about women and sport are disrupted. She shows us how to move forward. This is the power of storytelling."
– Norman K. Denzin, Ph.D., University of Illinois at Urbana-Champaign

To my family, who nurtured my writing efforts and raised me to love language and stories. To SBL, my first and last reader, whose faith in my capabilities far exceeds my own. And to Stuart Hall (1932–2014), Norman Denzin and Laurel Richardson for being the kinds of writers, change-makers and academics I can only aspire to be.

TABLE OF CONTENTS

PREFACE

Set in the near future, *Terra Ludus* follows a group of friends as their lives are turned upside down by the downstream effects of the actions of the protagonist, Daniela Bartoli.

Five years after the professional International Women's Basketball League is unceremoniously dumped by its parent men's organization, Daniela is working in Los Angeles as a freelance journalist and playing regular weekend pick-up games with her four friends, Mike, Constantin, Dominic and Simeon.

Her relatively simple life changes almost overnight after her vlog, challenging a powerful media corporation to step up and broadcast women's basketball, goes viral. The publicity sets off a chain reaction that brings the sport back into international prominence. As the public 'face' of the new competition, Daniela is sucked into a vortex of media and public visibility that leads her to question what is really important.

In an imagined context where all professional sport takes place in a single country – something like a permanent Olympic Games – we follow a cast of characters with very different viewpoints on a roller-coaster, year-long, journey as they adjust to the new women's league.

Terra Ludus explores the many and contradictory ways that gender, media and sport infuse our lives. In the face of dumbed-down and click-bait driven mainstream news delivery, it also challenges us to think about the possible implications of profit-driven media engagements with professional sport.

Ultimately, *Terra Ludus* is a story of unusual connections, budding possibilities, and what can happen when dominant ideas about women and sport are challenged and disrupted.

ABOUT THIS BOOK

The triggers for the novel emerge from my experiences as a sports reporter, sports columnist and academic who has been writing, researching and theorizing about media coverage of women's sport for more than 30 years. The 'ground' on which the action takes place is the sport of basketball, in large part because it is the sport with which I am most familiar, as a former player, referee and occasional coach. I also acknowledge that I am writing from a particular location, informed by more than a decade living in the United States, and from a lifetime in a land that made space for my ancestors through the signing of Te Tiriti o Waitangi/the Treaty of Waitangi in 1840, a pivotal moment in Aotearoa's history at which my great-great-grandfather is reputed to have been present (Death at, 1937). I attempt to honor my own and others' cultural and linguistic heritage through acknowledging the first peoples of both lands and by including both the English and Māori languages. However, *Terra Ludus* is not auto-ethnography, nor does it contain significant autobiographical elements. At its heart, it is an imagined world in which contradictory discourses collide and effloresce into new patterns that disrupt traditional ways of understanding the place of women in sport and media.

Terra Ludus is my response to the spectacular failure of sport studies scholars and activists to convince the mainstream sports media to increase coverage of women's sport. Over the last quarter century at least, it has become clear that, in Larry Grossberg's terms (see Liang et al., 2005), feminist sport scholars are not playing the right game, they are not playing on the right field, nor do they understand what's happening well enough. Indeed, if Albert Einstein was correct in arguing that the definition of insanity is doing the same thing repeatedly and expecting a different result, then those arguing for more coverage of women's sport could indeed be considered to be insane (Bruce & Hardin, 2014). For this is what activists, athletes and researchers have been doing for the past 30 years at least, producing thousands of studies documenting the persistent media ignoring of women's sport, preparing guidelines, complaining in letters to the editor, posting comments, writing blogs and placing their research before the world's sports media journalists and editors. And what has changed? Very little. Everyday news coverage of sportswomen languishes at about 10 per cent throughout much of the Western world, increasing for brief periods during major events such as the Olympic and Commonwealth Games or certain world championships, when nationalism becomes more important than gender in determining who or what counts as important (Bruce, Hovden, & Markula, 2010; Horky & Nieland, 2013; Jorgensen, 2005). This is not to deny that pockets of good practice exist, nor that some women's sports have successfully cracked the code. Professional tennis, especially the four Grand Slam tournaments, is one example, along with the predominantly female sport of netball in New Zealand, and the Women's National Basketball League (WNBA) in the United States, although basketball's current success follows at least two previous failed leagues.

In some contexts, the threads that have long woven femininity and physical frailty together have frayed to the point where strong, physically competent sportswomen have become *the* ideal of femininity (Bruce, 2016; Daniels & Wartena, 2011; Heywood & Dworkin, 2003). But overall, the big picture is dismal and shows little sign of forward progress. Indeed, in the 21st century, 'everyday sexism' continues to infuse media coverage, and there are indications of regression rather than progression (Cooky, Messner, & Hextrum, 2013).

In thinking through my own work and that of colleagues around the world, I realized that if academics want to make a difference, then we need to take seriously Grossberg's (1992) argument that, "We have to look at how both domination and subordination are lived, organized and resisted; we have to understand the possibilities of subordination that are open and allowed within the structures of domination, and perhaps point beyond them" (p. 67). He suggests that "by gaining a better sense of the state of play on the field of forces in popular culture and daily life, perhaps we can see more clearly where struggles are possible and, in some cases, even actual. Then we can try to find ways to oppose them, or help articulate them, to nurture and support them and perhaps, to bring them into visible relations with other struggles" (p. 66).

Through refusing to accept sporting discourses that have historically disempowered sportswomen, the characters in *Terra Ludus* reveal the limits (and stupidities) of those discourses, while creating other connections. In this approach, the novel is informed by third wave feminism, which rejects the historic *either/or* articulation that culturally constructs sportswomen as *either* physically competent *or* feminine. Instead, it recognizes the contradictions and complexities of 21st century female embodiment, presenting female athletes who see no contradiction between femininity and physicality and refuse to 'play the game' as it has been constructed for them (Bruce, 2016). Instead, they chart their own paths, write their own (new) stories and, hopefully, entice you, the reader, along for the ride.

THE AUDIENCE

This novel is appropriate as supplemental reading in a range of courses in sport studies, media studies, cultural studies, communication, journalism, gender studies, sociology, creative writing, performance, and physical education, or can be read entirely for pleasure by anyone interested in gender, media and sport.

REFERENCES

Bruce, T. (2016). New rules for new times: Sportswomen and media representation in the third wave. *Sex Roles, 74,* 361–376.

Bruce, T., & Hardin, M. (2014). Reclaiming our voices: Sportswomen and social media. In A. C. Billings & M. Hardin (Eds.), *Routledge handbook of sport and new media* (pp. 311–319). New York, NY: Routledge.

Bruce, T., Hovden, J., & Markula, P. (Eds.). (2010). *Sportswomen at the olympics: A global comparison of newspaper coverage.* Rotterdam: Sense Publishers.

Cooky, C., Messner, M. A., & Hextrum, R. H. (2013). Women play sport, but not on TV: A longitudinal study of televised news media. *Communication & Sport, 1*(3), 203–230. doi:10.1177/2167479513476947

Daniels, E. A., & Wartena, H. (2011). Athlete or sex symbol: What boys think of media representations of female athletes. *Sex Roles, 65*(7–8), 566–579.

Death at 93. (1937, April 13). *The New Zealand Herald,* p. 12.

Grossberg, L. (1992). *We gotta get out of this place: Popular conservatism and postmodern culture.* New York, NY: Routledge.

Heywood, L., & Dworkin, S. L. (2003). *Built to win: The female athlete as cultural icon.* Minneapolis, MN: University of Minnesota Press.

Horky, T., & Nieland, J-U. (2013). Comparing sports reporting from around the world: Numbers and facts on sports in daily newspapers. In T. Horky & J-U. Nieland (Eds.), *International sports press survey 2011.* Norderstedt, Germany: Books on Demand GmbH.

Jorgensen, S. S. (2005, October 31). The world's best advertising agency: The sports press. *Mandagmorgen* [Mondaymorning], *37,* 1–7.

Liang, X., Wong, P., Wong, H-W., & Chan, S-H. (2005, June). *Let's tell a different story: An interview with Lawrence Grossberg.* Lingnan University, Hong Kong. Retrieved from http://www.ln.edu.hk/mcsln/3rd_issue/interview_01.htm

ACKNOWLEDGEMENTS

This novel would not have been possible without the support and advice of many people. First, I acknowledge Paul Cowan, Margaret Henley, Katene Paenga, Ma Zhao, Steve Leichtweis, Jen Rankine and Travis Bull for specialist advice on specific elements of the novel. Any errors are entirely mine.

Thanks also my friends and whānau who read early drafts and gave me valuable feedback, including Bobbie Whiting, Richard Bruce, Chris Leichtweis, Nicoletta Rata, Esther Fitzpatrick, Katie Fitzpatrick, Tony Tapsell, Odette Miller-Waugh, Deborah Fraser, Fetaui Isoefo, and Dale Hills. I am fortunate to belong to the Narrative and Metaphor Special Interest Network (NAMSIN) at the Faculty of Education and Social Work, which promotes and supports creative writing practice. I also thank the Faculty for providing financial support to employ Diane Osborne of Design Options to format the novel.

Deep gratitude goes to my friend and writing buddy Victoria Paraschak with whom I shared the intense joy and challenge of writing 50,000 words in 30 days during National Novel Writing Month (http://nanowrimo.org/). The work I produced forms the core of *Terra Ludus*. During NaNoWriMo, I was inspired and reassured by advice from published authors Catherynne Valente, Veronica Roth, Jeff VanderMeer, Malinda Lo and Rainbow Rowell, who blogged throughout the month. Like Rowell, I was "shocked" that "I kept almost every word I wrote during NaNoWriMo". My thanks also go to the Auckland region NaNoWriMo-ers, whose interest in sci-fi writing inspired me to set the novel a few years in the future.

Finally, I want to acknowledge Laurel Richardson for bringing the Sense Social Fictions series to my attention, Patricia Leavy and Shalen Lowell, and the team at Sense Publishers, without whom the opportunity to bring creative, research-informed writing to life would be much more challenging. To those at Sense who have supported this novel into publication – Peter de Liefde, Paul Chambers, Jolanda Karada, Robert van Gameren, and Edwin Bakker – thank you.

CHAPTER 1

END OF AN ERA

The sound of the buzzer ripped through the roar of the crowd, creating a millisecond of silence as everyone realized it was over. Then the rolling roar began again. Bodies poured off the bench onto the wooden floor, leaping, embracing, screaming with joy.

Daniela was bowled to the ground by an over-boisterous tackle. *Gaia, that hurt,* she thought as her elbow took the brunt of the fall. *But who cares? We won!* As she heaved her way out of the pile of sweaty females, Denise's voice penetrated through the noise.

"Danny! Danny! Where's Danny?"

"Over here," she yelled and ran towards her co-captain. A foot apart, they both paused, face to face. Then they stepped forward simultaneously and began their trademark low-five, high-five hand slap, one side then the other. Rotating to stand back-to-back, they repeated the move, before rotating again to grab each other in a fierce hug. They rejoined the roiling mass of players, coaches and support staff still reveling in their success.

As the hubbub died down a bit, the team gathered together, walking the edge of the court blowing kisses, waving and bowing their thanks to their vociferous fans, before venturing into the crowd to hug family or close friends.

They were champions. Again.

As the organizers got the court ready for the medals ceremony, Danny approached the Terra Sparta bench, stopping to shake hands or commiserate. They'd played their hearts out to no avail, as Canestri Mulier's stifling defense and Danny's last-second heroics shut them out.

Twenty minutes later, adorned in champions t-shirts and medals, they headed to the locker room to wash off their rapidly cooling sweat and begin the celebrating in earnest. Danny set her Most Valuable

Player trophy beside her locker, giving it a tender caress before hitting the showers. When she returned, wrapped only in her Canestri Mulier towel, it was sitting alongside the winner's trophy on the table in the middle of the room, most of the team ranged around both trophies in a semi-circle.

Oh no. Here we go.

Denise stepped forward, recreating the medal ceremony, drawling in her best announcer voice. "And here, ladies and gentlemen, we have Daniela Bartoli, this year's MVP and the League's only Living Legend. And may I say what a marvelous finals series she had. Let us enumerate her myriad of skills. First, she dominated the high post – being, of course, far too short and too scared to mix it up with us big girls in the middle." Giggles all around, as the taller players high-fived. "Second, her basketball smarts meant she led the series and the season in assists. Oh what a selfless player." Again the friendly sarcasm triggered a wave of giggles. "Third, she shot the lights out with remarkable consistency – maybe due to those genetic enhancements she received in the off-season?"

"I call lies on that one," Danny interjected. "You all know if I did that, none of you would ever get to score a point!" She high-fived the nearest teammate, flicking a triumphant look Denise's way.

Undeterred, Denise continued to the climax, accompanied by rhythmic clapping that built in speed and intensity. "Fourth, she did enough convincing renditions of being fouled, including that textbook charge that won us the game, to earn this year's butt-on-the-floor award. And finally, dear fans, we can't forget that Ms Bartoli also topped the ratings in fouls. Aggressive little minx isn't she? And, on behalf of everyone in the team, can I say that I'm mightily happy that I play *with* her, rather than against those unnaturally sharp elbows."

Knowing what was now expected, Danny bowed to her teammates and initiated the team dance as Shania Twain's 'Man I Feel Like a Woman' rang through the changing area. Then they were all dancing in unison, singing the first verse with uninhibited enthusiasm.

As the MVP-winner, Danny's responsibility was to sing the chorus by herself. So she belted it out, hoping that volume would compensate for her lack of melody. As she sang the team's own variation – "All flirts, short skirts" – she hitched up her towel to mini-skirt length and did a twirl, before finishing on the title line of the song.

Then the whole team hollered and whooped their way through the second verse. As their coaches and support staff entered the room, they greeted them with a final full chorus, hoisting both trophies high, nothing but happiness and anticipation of the partying to come in their voices.

As they passed around the champagne-filled winner's trophy, their coach Roselyn Smyth raised her voice above the laughter and chatter.

"Hey girls," she said, swapping high fives with the closest players. "Time to quieten down a bit. Sit down if you don't mind."

Expecting the standard congratulations, they took a few minutes to find their places on the hard benches in front of the lockers.

"What's up coach?" Denise asked, still smiling. "You're not looking too happy. Is something wrong?"

At her words, most players focused their attention. Silence rippled over the group as, one by one, they absorbed the serious facial expressions of everyone on their support crew. Danny thought she saw tears in the eyes of their physio, just before she turned away, apparently looking for a place to sit. *Gaia. Something is going on. Could Roselyn have been fired? Surely not. We just won the championship.*

Roselyn stayed standing, making eye contact with every player, her smile a shadow of those arrayed in front of her. "Well girls. Let me first say you did an outstanding job tonight. That was the best ball I've seen you play all season, and you needed every bit of skill and guile and smarts to win that match. You made me proud and you should be proud of yourselves as well."

"Yeah. True that," emphasized Denise, her statement followed by cheers from the players. "And on behalf of my co-captain Danny and the team, I want to thank you for what you've done for us … and to us," she added ruefully. "I've never run so much in my life. And I hated it, almost every minute of it. But," and she looked for agreement from the rest of the players, "we needed every bit of that fitness tonight. All that hard work really paid off." More clapping, high-fives and cheers ensued.

"Thanks Denise, thanks Danny, and thanks all of you. I truly appreciate it. I know you didn't always agree with my tactics. I know you didn't always like the training I put you through but I hope tonight you know it was all worth it. To win this championship."

Another round of cheers followed her statement but they died out quickly as the players realized there was more to come.

"And that's the good news. That we won. That you won and that Danny took out the MVP. But I have some other news to share and it's not good."

"You haven't been fired have you?" Danny burst out. "That wouldn't be fair." Yeahs of support from the other players.

"Not exactly," came the response, "but I have some sad news. And I'm very sorry to be telling you now but I want you to hear it from me and not through Int-TV or social media."

"Hear what? What's going on?" Danny question sounded more like a demand.

"The league," she said. "It's the league. You won the championship tonight and you should savor it." She paused to take in and release a deep breath. "Because this is the last championship ever."

Ever? What does that mean? Ever?

"Because of the international economic situation, the Basketball Association International has decided to cancel the women's...."

She didn't get any further before Denise erupted to her feet. "Cancel the league? Cancel the league! You can't be serious."

"Unbelievably I am serious. Or at least they are. They say that women's basketball isn't financially viable and..."

This time it was Danny who interrupted, her voice barely audible over the confused babble that now filled the room. "But the stadium was packed tonight, and we're all over social media. We have insanely committed fan vloggers. What do they mean it's not viable?"

"I don't know Danny, I'm sorry. All I know is that right after the game, we were told that the league has been cancelled permanently."

Confusion began to shift to anger as players turned to those near them. Disconnected phrases swirled. "Cancelled?" "It's our league, not theirs." "Permanently?" "For why?" "They can't do that!" "No fair." "That's total b.s." "Who do they think they are?"

"I know. I know," said Roselyn. "And I'm very sorry."

Danny was now on her feet, her right forefinger drawing a circle encompassing the entire group. "But where will we play? Terra Ludus is all there is for pro ball these days.

"I don't know. I don't have any answers."

"But what does it mean for us? For you? For everyone?" Denise demanded.

"It means that all of us will be paid out the minimum remaining on our contracts – that's to the end of next month."

"And then what?"

"And then we all go home," Roselyn responded as her shoulders slumped and she collapsed into a chair, tears finally flowing. "Home to where ever home is."

REAL LIFE?

Even now, five years later, most people see Danny as one of the lucky ones. After all, she got to live on Terra Ludus. She got to live the dream, just like her father. Of course, they don't know what it's really like. All they see is the surface, the excitement produced for mass consumption by Internet TV. And from that perspective, it looks like paradise. Lush fields, mesmerizing emerald-green water, and skies of blue so vivid and clear they seem photo-shopped. Fast roads and fancy cars. Fresh water, free-range organic meat, and land-grown fruit and vegetables. All the latest technology. And the clothes. Whatever is new, they're wearing it. The action never stops. It's exciting, physically challenging, and highly competitive. Life is lived large and loud.

But that's only half the story. Danny knows that's what Intviewers don't understand. They don't see the boredom, the insecurity, the disparities in resources between different sports and teams. They can't imagine the feeling when your dream ends without warning, and you find yourself back home, looking in from the outside.

And that's where most people are. On the outside. Compelled, like the worst form of addiction, to seek their daily pleasure, their faux intimacy, their birds-eye view of the action. Because that's what the northern island of this small nation has become. A global Internet sport reality show.

The shift happened in the mid-2000s, as media corporations tasted the possibilities of tax breaks, free state-of-the-art facilities, and a stable government with secure borders. By the time the major nations realized what was happening, it was too late. Internet media had found a profitable and sympathetic host and thereafter persuaded professional sports leagues to turn their temporary off-season training bases into permanent homes, supplied with world-class medical treatment, cutting edge equipment, clean air and water, and meat grown on the land rather than in a test-tube. As fuel shortages moved air travel out of the price range of ordinary citizens, media corporations exploited their ability to sell vicarious involvement in sport for even greater profits.

Terra Ludus started out as a media nickname created by a sports journalist trying to establish his literary credentials. Harking back to a mythic past seemed quite reasonable in the face of escalating political conflict, food insecurity, forced migration, and pandemics caused by over-population and porous national borders. Somehow, it went viral, the marketers got on board, and then all the sports took on Latin names.

Basketball became Canestri, American football rebadged itself Craticula, rugby union chose Harpastan, cricket settled on Gryllus, ice hockey adopted Glaciem, on and on ad nauseum. And the changes stuck. Even the southern island of Aotearoa, renowned in its own right as a spectacular outdoor adventureland, renamed itself Terra Periculum, the Place of Encountering Risks. Many other nations reimagined themselves, even if unofficially, through adopting a Latin moniker.

So that's Terra Ludus, the Land of Sport. A real place but not really real, if that makes sense. From the sport fan perspective, there's Terra Ludus and then there's Terra Everywhere-Else.

Not that Terra Ludus is completely immune from real problems. Even though it's well away from the major nations, Int-Rads regularly and successfully damage the undersea Internet cables, creating enough chaos that there's never quite enough bandwidth for all the teams, let alone native Terra Ludans. Danny has to use old-school technology (like the Web for Gaia's sake) just to stay in touch. Canestri Mulier, the only semi-professional women's basketball team left on TL, can't afford the bandwidth to provide virtual contact, let alone augmented reality experiences. Danny's father gets to take his annual online immersive 'walk around' with the Harpastans to see how things are going but Danny has to rely on the Canestri Mulier vlog and buffered low-spec vid streams.

They've repaired the cable more than a dozen times in the last decade but it goes down again within months, sometimes weeks. On top of that, net neutrality no longer exists, trampled to death under the drive for profits. Once governments allowed the merger and consolidation of media corporations and Internet service providers, the new mega-corps quickly moved to artificially throttle access, creating two-tiered Int delivery. Now it's only global corporations and the wealthy who can afford 'fast lane' access. Everyone else is stuck in the slow lane, constantly making choices between quality and quantity.

So even though the Int was supposed to be a liberator, it just seems to reinforce the haves and have-nots, even among the sports teams. Int access is the oil of this century, and bandwidth and cables are just as vulnerable and important as oil pipelines were last century.

FRIENDS

Four of Danny's best friends organize their lives around the Terra Ludus schedule of programming. They don't watch everything – it's available 24-hours a day on multiple streams – but they have enough favorites that it's a challenge to extract them from their muscle-massaging chairs to actually spend significant time outside, in nature, with the wind and sun and rain. A few years ago, even convincing them to pick up a basketball and shoot a few hoops took some doing. That might be because they're guys who still resist the idea that Danny can seriously kick their asses on a basketball court, but they even avoid the other sports they played. Most of the time they'd rather watch the Terra Ludans run and leap and carve their way through the water, round the rims or down the slopes.

She still doesn't get that. She'd much rather do it herself than watch someone else. She can't figure out what is so endlessly fascinating. But that is the seduction that is Int-TV. It's brighter, faster, bigger, closer. And there's popcorn washed down by cold beer from the couch cooler.

Mike, whose belly is incrementally obscuring his formerly sculpted abdominal muscles, is the worst. Since she got back from TL, he refuses to go anywhere near a basketball court, even though he used to play regularly with the other guys. Just yesterday, as she, Simeon, Constantin and Dominic walked out the door to play pick-up, he sneered at them.

"What are you doing? Don't bother with that inferior shit. The real stuff's right here."

But, instead of challenging him, the guys just shuffled out the door, none of them willing to make eye contact or stand up to Mike's put down. Even Danny's attempt to shut Mike up, by suggesting that moving might help get rid of his spare tire, didn't stop him.

"It's pretty fit underneath that layer of fat," he responded, tenderly patting his stomach. "The muscles are there. I've just got a 12 pack instead of a six pack over the top of them." They exited to his bark of laughter.

And Simeon told her they never reveal to their other friends that Danny is a 'girl'. "It's a good thing your nickname's Danny," he said. "It makes you sound like a guy. So we can still talk about the game and how many points you made and how much you showed us up without looking like sissies."

At the time, she wondered what she was supposed to do with that comment. She didn't have any kind of response ready so didn't say anything. But she still wonders. What's the problem with being beaten by a girl? Surely skill is what matters. It's what matters to her. And it's why she mostly plays with guys.

That's the problem with spending time on Terra Ludus. You can't get there unless you've already got skills, and being there takes you to whatever peak you're capable of achieving. And that's exactly what happened for Danny. Some players couldn't handle the intensive training or the limited contact with home, and quickly left or were kicked out, but most took advantage of the opportunity and put up with the claustrophobic and one-dimensional focus that accompanied it. Visitors and sponsors seldom found their way to her part of the island so money was tight but they worked hard and played hard. She was part of it. Like all the sports, it was hierarchical and if you didn't play politics in the right way, it was difficult to feel secure. But Danny couldn't bring herself to play those kinds of games. She wanted to be respected on merit. Her strategy worked for nearly a decade until, at only 25, she and all her teammates were on a flight out of there, along with every other team in the professional women's league. Now there's only Canestri Mulier left on the island, serving as TL's de facto national team, competing in the Terra Australia league.

It wasn't until she arrived back in Terra Altrix that Danny realized how tense she was, how much she had been living on adrenaline and tension. It took months to re-learn how to relax, to breathe freely, to dislodge the burning ball of acid that flourished in her gut. She can't imagine ever wanting to live on Terra Ludus again.

The league's sudden demise still hurts too much, and many of her friends have moved on as well.

But the upshot is that Danny is still better than most women although she has a crew of former Terra Ludus players that she sometimes plays social pick-up with. But on Saturdays, it's the guys who are prepared to take her on at one of the small courts scattered across the city. Danny often ends up bruised but that pain is something she still craves. And, even if she says so herself, she still has a super-sweet jump shot and a nifty dodge to get open for it. At six feet tall, she's the shortest, but they can hardly ever stop her. Maybe because, just like her, they're all a step slower than they used to be.

"Manu!" Danny's shout rang out, disrupting Dominic's shot, as she abandoned the game and ran towards the gate that restricted entry to local residents.

Disturbed by her breach of basketball etiquette, and Dom's unexpected miss, the 2-on-2 game came to a halt and three male faces turned to watch her progress. Oblivious, Danny had already reached the gate.

"What are you doing here?"

"Picked up some work at the last minute so thought I better check up on you Cuz," came the reply as Danny punched in the keypad numbers by feel and swung the gate open. The artificial barrier gone, Manu and Danny leaned towards each other, touching foreheads and noses, sharing the breath of life for long seconds.

"Cuz?" queried Con to the others as they casually bounced the ball back and forth between them.

"And what's that they're doing?" responded Dominic. "Who in Gaia is he? I've never seen him before."

As they wondered, Manu swept Danny up in hug and swung her around in circles as her unrestrained laughter carried back to them. Then a yelp of surprise as he swung her over his shoulder in a fireman's carry, followed by helpless giggles as he transported her back to the game.

"Hey guys, "she said from upside down. "This is Manu, from Terra Ludus, an old friend."

"And her cousin," Manu added, returning her to an upright position and slinging one arm across her shoulders, before offering his hand in friendship to Con, standing closest.

'Cousin?" queried Con as he accepted the handshake. "You don't look much alike. I'm Con by the way."

"Well, looks can be deceiving, bro." Manu's cheeky smile indicated he wasn't going to enlighten the guys so Danny stepped into the breach.

"That's Dominic," she said, pointing to her left, "and over there is Simeon with the ball. They're my Saturday crew. You've heard me talk about them. As for cousin, it's not a blood thing. I played ball with his sister and Manu's whānau looked after me when I first arrived on TL."

"Far-no?" queried Dom, moving forward to shake Manu's hand. "And what was that thing you just did?"

"Whānau is our word for family, and that was a hongi. It's our traditional way of greeting each other, "Manu explained. "As for her, she turned out to be OK, had a bit of brown in her, so we informally adopted her. We call it whāngai. In her case it's not legal or anything but it runs deep."

"You're not joking," Danny agreed, lightly punching him on the arm. "Once you're in, you can never escape. They can find you anywhere. Which, by the way, raises the question of exactly how you did find me, and how come I didn't know you were coming."

"Last minute Cuz. And the Aunties know where you live. When you didn't answer the door, I knew I'd find you on the nearest court. And here you are."

"Wanna join us? Just like old times?"

Worried looks crossed the guys' faces. Although they were all well over six feet, Manu wasn't much shorter, and he had powerful shoulders and big hands. And something about the way he moved suggested he might know his way around a court.

"Nah, Cuz. Not dressed for it. And I'm carrying a bit of a shoulder injury from Worlds. You go ahead. I always liked watching you play. Be nice to see if you've still got it." He caught the flicker in her eyes and knew she'd respond to the challenge. And she decided to let the guys out of their misery.

"He doesn't mean basketball," she said. "He means waka ama world champs. You know, outrigger canoeing. But he's not a bad baller either. His marae has its own court and everyone plays after a fashion. Even some of the kuia still have pretty sweet shots, and they're not afraid to tell you what you're doing wrong."

The fleeting smile of memory was chased by a shadow of loss as she shrugged off his arm and gestured for the ball. "I miss that actually. You know, just turning up and there'd always be someone to play with." The smile returned as she addressed the guys. "And you never knew who it would be. Could be anyone from 8 to 80. You just played to the conditions. As for him," nodding towards Manu, as she slotted a lazy two-point shot, "He threw it all away to paddle around as an insignificant speck on the ocean. But he's not too bad at it. Got a few medals to show for it."

"You could have been good too, if you'd bothered," was Manu's quick comeback. He turned to the guys, "But she's barely average at waka ama. Threw it all away to chase a ball around a little indoor court." Conspiratorially, he looked at them. "I wonder if she's still competent after a few years away from the big time."

"No doubt about it," Simeon spoke for the first time. "She usually kicks our asses."

"I call bullshit on that," replied Dom. "C'mon Con, let's show him how it's done in our part of the world."

Reacting to the flashing light on his wrist, Manu apologised. "Aroha mai. Sorry I can't stay to see it, but work calls. Ka kite anō. See you later." He mimed vidding Danny before nimbly vaulting the gate. The last they saw was his koru-patterned Hawaiian shirt disappearing behind the trees that surrounded the court.

"Had your little fun?" was Mike's sarcastic greeting as they returned, plastered in sweat and grinning.

"Got to keep Danny happy," Simeon replied. "She needs her weekly fix."

But she knows, and they know she knows, that this is sophistry. Deep down in that secret place in their hearts, they know that doing it for themselves is important because it connects them to themselves and to each other in deep ways. But that doesn't mean they can acknowledge it publicly. Danny assumes it's some weird guy thing where their masculinity is compromised if they admit to Mike that they love it, that they wouldn't miss the weekly match-ups. Or that Danny is the best one on the court. What she doesn't get is that they won't watch women's basketball at all. On the rare times it's on, and the even rarer times like today when her old team, Canestri Mulier, is playing, they switch to another channel, to something stupid like football.

"But it's boring," Mike grumbled. "It's slow and they can't dunk, and they pass the ball too much."

"So you could beat them I suppose?" she retorted.

"Of course. Chicks can't play ball," Mike said, to nods of agreement from the others. When Danny raised her eyebrows, he backtracked a bit. "Well, you can of course. And you could even back in high school," he conceded. "But most of them can't."

"Those women can seriously play," she proposed. "Even if they're semi-pro, with all the new systems, the level is constantly improving. It's great." She could hear her voice rising. "And what's wrong with lots of passing? That's clever play. It sets up openings for a clean shot."

"Clean shot! Clean shot!" Mike threw his arms up in exasperation, sloshing beer on his t-shirt. "Who the hell wants a clean shot? Give me some action. I wanna see bodies on the floor."

"But that's only one aspect of the game," she persisted. But it is too late. She's lost him, and the other three sit there either pretending they're not even in the room or sniggering as this old argument goes round and round.

SPEAKING OUT

Danny posted the vid the next day. She decided to go formal. She dressed up (or down given the amount of cleavage on show), slapped on the lippy, dug out the mascara and applied a bit of hair gel to enhance her short cut. Sent it direct to the National Broadcasting Board President and posted it on sportsfreak.tl.oceanworld, the most women's-sport-friendly website. Emailed the link to the women's International Federation and the current Canestri Mulier coach and suggested she forward it to the Terra Ludus and Terra Australia League HQs. She kept it under three minutes to reduce bandwidth charges.

"Dear National Broadcasting Board. It has come to my attention that you are not meeting your statutory obligations. I'm sure you see this as something you would want to address immediately and I have a solution. As you may be aware, men's sport hogs all the bandwidth. So much so that clickers have been conditioned to think that's the only form of sport that exists. Your charter says you must provide diversity, showing the full range of people and activities. In the last review, many people said they wanted more diversity in sports programming. So here's the deal. Basketball is the highest participation sport in Terra Altrix, and more women play basketball than any other sport. I'm a former Canestri Mulier ludio and I know there's a vast untapped and desiring audience out there for women's basketball. Your audience for sport is falling – the public data shows this. You need new audiences. And women (currently a measly 25% of clickers, and only 15% of bandwidth hoggers) are your growth area. Why don't you commit some resources to women's basketball? Let's say one game a week to start with, every week, close to prime time, tagged to the men's game (preferably before, because many of your potential viewers will be mothers who need to get to sleep at a reasonable time). I'm sure I can get a group of ex-players and fans together to create a supporting site, to vlog and produce Vid to help create some hype. Now I know what you'll say. Nobody wants to watch women. But have you ever asked yourself why? No, it's not because they're no good. No, it's not because the men are faster, jump higher, or are more aggressive. It's because you haven't given them a chance. Men's sport didn't start out popular. It was an audience that had to be built. It was created out of nothing by journalists paid to promote it. Well, here's your chance to get in on the ground floor of something amazing. Women's basketball is not the same as men's. It has a different style – more passing, more strategy, more interesting – and you could build that into the promotion. I can hook you up with whomever you need. And the women are good people. You won't be dealing with bad publicity all the time. No sex or betting scandals. No illegal genetic enhancements. No drug rings. No racism. No domestic violence. No homophobia. Come on NBB. Meet your obligations and make money by bringing in new advertisers – ones who want to market to different audiences. The men will come around. They love sport and once they have a chance to see the women's game, to be educated about its intricacies, to know the athletes and teams, they'll be as enthusiastic as you could ever want. So, come on. Be the leader you can and should be. Don't just follow the pack. Lock in a long-term contract and reap the rewards. Looking forward to talking with you. Signing off, Daniela Bartoli.

She didn't have any real hopes it would make a difference. But yesterday's conversation rubbed away at her, in a place that was always slightly reddened and sometimes openly raw. So, like an irritant in an oyster, she worked at it, and the vid was her pearl, the only thing she could think of doing. And that was that.

Simeon was the first to ping her, 24 hours later, via her personal vid link. "Hey girl. That was some rant," he started. "Everyone's talking about it."

"What rant? The one at Mike's? Who's everybody?" She was sitting at the kitchen bench in her sweaty workout gear about to take a sip of chai latte.

"No, silly woman. Your vid. The one you posted on sportsfreak. It's going viral. People are sending it all over. You've got a thousand comments and 15 vid responses already. Not bad. Not bad."

Her heart sank. *Uh oh.* "And what are they saying?"

"Oh, you know. The usual. Mostly anti but some surprising support. The marketing manager for the men's league even posted a short vid saying the League thought it was a good idea."

"Really?" A bubble of hope rose.

"Yeah. Well, all he can see is money. As long as they don't cut the men's coverage, then it's all good for Canestri I guess."

She could see Simeon laughing while staring at another vid screen. His unique snuffling rumble suffused her kitchen. "You gotta see this one," he said. "Gaia. Some people have nothing better to do with their time." He looked up to check for her nod of approval.

"Right. Here's the funniest one I've read so far. Not a vid though, just a post. Got to be a guy. Calls himself hoopfantastico. "This Daniela hag should just shut up and get herself a real man. That'd sort her out. She's clearly delusional if she thinks any real man would want to watch women play the best game in the world."

Just as she was thinking it sounded a lot like Mike, Simeon voiced the same thought. "Could be Mike maybe. Making a joke?"

"I don't think so. I hope not," she said. "He'd say it to my face, not via some anonymous public post."

"Well here's the end of it," Simeon went on. "NBB. Listen up. Don't pay any attention to her. I, and I'm sure all other red-blooded men, will give up their subscriptions if you start broadcasting second-rate rubbish. And then where would you be? Signing off in support of only showing the best there is."

The bubble of hope collapsed in on itself, replaced by a wash of nausea.

"Anyway, you ought to check them out. And don't worry about the bozos like this guy. He's clearly never seen a women's game. He's just spouting the party line. Must have a small penis."

She laughed. She was surprised to hear him speaking in support of the women's game, given the conversations they usually had at Mike's. Then she realized Simeon didn't participate in them directly. He didn't overtly agree with Mike or Constantin, the other main naysayer, but he'd never said anything supportive either. The ancient phrase *those who do nothing are equally culpable* sprang to mind, followed by *this is the first time he's taken a stand (sort of). And that's probably because hoops-idiot-bozo is attacking me.*

"Oi. Mars to Danny. Wake up. I think this is gonna be big so you better be ready. A lot of these posts have linked to other websites so it's getting out there. It's even gone off-world from what I can see. You're onto something." His eyes focused more closely on her. "And you better get dressed and do the girly thing. Nice look on the vid by the way. A bit different from on the court. I've got to go, work calls and all that. Good luck."

As the screen went blank, she checked the timeclock. Seventh hour. She was tempted to stay where she was, to peruse the comments and follow their links but she knows the danger of disappearing down the Int rabbit hole. And if he was right, she needed to be prepared, on all levels. Her armor shiny, her real self locked away safe from attack. If Simeon thought she managed the femme look on the vid, that's what she'd replicate today. It was stupid but might be necessary. Too many misconceptions about 'chummy' girls in her sport and it was too easy for the haters to dismiss the game because of that. So, in case she got any interview requests, she decided she'd do her best to visually disrupt their thinking, to play girly and dodge any questions about her own sexuality. Of course it might amount to nothing but a storm in a teacup. A flash of fury that would subside as quickly as it arose, while the Int-TV sportworld carried on uninterrupted.

At the start of ninth hour her work vid link pinged. The ID-tag said NBB. A jolt of fear stabbed deep in her chest. *Should I ignore it? No. I did the vid because this is what I believe. If I didn't want them to follow up I shouldn't have done it. And I did end by saying I looked forward to talking with them.* So she took a deep breath and opened the connection.

"Hello." A heart-shaped face appeared, atop shoulders clad in an elegant grey suit. *A woman. Older than me but ageless. Gorgeous.* Reactions raced by in staccato fashion. She must look like those cartoon vids of goldfish, or maybe a deer in the headlights (the phrase *an oldie but a goodie* irrationally skittered through her mind, especially given the fact that hardly anyone actually 'drives' a car anymore, let alone collides with wildlife. But it's one of her Dad's sayings from back in the day when self-driving was the dominant form of transport).

"Hello," she replied.

"Ah, you must be Daniela. I'm Imelda Consonati, head of programming for NBB. Nice to meet you."

"Hello." Danny said it again, disconcerted at Imelda's cool assessing gaze, and not sure how to continue.

"I was hoping to set up a face-to-face with you as soon as possible," Imelda said. "Are you available to zoom to us today?"

How to respond? If I say yes will I look too eager? Will I look like I don't have a real job with demands? (Which I don't really since I'm a freelance journalist and can work my own schedule.) Oh well. Nothing ventured, nothing gained (another oldie but still a goodie).

"Sure. I'd need to see what zoomers are available."

"Excellent. I was hoping you'd agree. And don't worry about the zoomer. I already have one booked for eleventh hour. It will take two hours to reach NBB headquarters and we'll have you back home by twenty-first hour."

"That sounds do-able. What would you like me to bring? Can you give me an idea what you want to discuss?" Thank Gaia her wits were starting to reassert themselves.

"We liked some of your suggestions and want to talk through some options with you. I don't really want to do it over vid, especially an unencrypted one. So why don't we wait until you arrive?"

"Alright," she said, just to vary her mostly monosyllabic responses. "What station do I need to be at, and what name is the ticket under?"

"Can you get to Union Station?" At Danny's nod, she continued. "So it will be Union Station to start, Mountain View to exit. I'll have an Escort waiting. And it is under your name. See you soon." And she sliced out.

Danny put a high definition vid link through to Simeon who opened it straightaway.

"Guess what?"

"Oh, I don't know. You got a date?" This was often his opening line.

21

"Actually I do," she replied. His irises expanded and his nostrils flared (the problem with high def vids these days is that you can see every little movement, blemish, hair, etc.). *Ah hah, that got him.* "A real date too. In Mountain View."

"Mountain View. You don't know anyone there." She just sat silently, smiling at him, waiting for him to figure it out.

It took almost a minute, a lot of bandwidth on a vid. Then, with a vigorous side-to-side, I'm-an-idiot, shake of his head, he burst out, "Mountain View. NBB." Looking for her reaction. "Really?" She nodded as he repeated the question, "Really? They want to talk to you?"

"Yep. And right now. I'm on a zoomer in less than two hours. Amazing huh?"

"Amazing ain't the word girl! Wow. That is seriously kick-ass." She could see him checking her out again. "Stand up," he ordered. "Do a twirl." She obliged, not worried that anyone else in the shared business-space would pay attention. Everyone here ran their own small operations and they generally didn't interact except on a superficial level.

"You'll do. Actually you don't look too shabby when you make an effort."

"That kind of flattery will get you everywhere," she laughed.

"No. Seriously. You look really good. Professional but femme. That outfit reads I'm focused but friendly, which is what you want."

"Since when did you become my fashion consultant?" This was a side of Simeon she'd never seen in the confines their usual on-court or five-around-the-Int-TV gatherings.

"Since you needed one," he responded. "And you need one now methinks." His grin was enough to show he wasn't criticizing. "But you'll do. Good luck. Let me know how it goes."

"Will do. Over and out." And she sliced the link. As she sat back, it occurred to her to wonder why he was the first person she contacted. Not her parents or best girlfriends Vicky or Nancy. He's the one who gets it, she realized. He knows sport, he knows business, and he knows me. Dad knows sport but he's retired and he never experienced life at the bottom of the sporting hierarchy. And he played before the Int era. Vic and Nancy wouldn't really understand. They aren't sports fans. They barely even know how to score in tennis.

Anyway, the vid hook up was calming and, surprisingly, left her feeling that she really could do this. Maybe, just maybe, her vid might lead to something good. It couldn't hurt anyway.

There was no point trying to work on her current story about the scientists attempting to set up a self-sustaining cockroach colony on Mars, she put her icom to sleep, stashed it in her bag, grabbed her coat, caught the local Metro Expo to downtown, and walked the short distance to a coffee shop in the Z-station with her favorite thinking tools, a paper notebook and pen. She knows it's old-fashioned, even archaic, but she's a doodler and a concept-mapper and has always liked thinking with an actual rather than virtual pen in hand. She figured that an hour of mapping out her arguments would help. Then she'd review her vid and use the free Int access on the zoomer to read the responses so she'd know what the resistance points were likely to be. She hadn't read any yet because she'd wanted to make some progress on the Mars story. In fact she hadn't even opened her personal me-mail or business wor-mail to avoid being distracted.

The coffee shop was a chain. Stark white walls reflected light, with the main warmth coming in the form of well-worn, red leather booths replete with docking ports, squishy cushions and, what Danny liked most, a no-music and no-public-vid policy. Blessed silence except for the whoosh of the espresso machine and occasional bursts of conversation. It was early enough in the day that she scored a desirable booth next to a window. With a Terra Sparta eggnog chai for brain fuel, she began outlining her main argument. What would convince NBB that there was not only public good but financial profit in broadcasting women's basketball? Who were her main basketball contacts and who did they know who would get behind the project? She'd need to be able to suggest some ex-players or coaches as potential commentators, to recruit a group of fans to write regular blogs and some willing to put their faces out there on vlogs. She'd have to do this herself too, even though she was still angry about the international women's league being cut so unceremoniously.

Gaia! There was a lot to think about. It had never occurred to her that this might be possible. But billions of people already invest their emotions, energy, and bandwidth following players or teams that they're unlikely ever to meet in person, because the cost of getting to Terra Ludus is out of reach for most people, and access to the popular teams is so carefully controlled.

Danny doesn't really understand what's so endlessly fascinating about Int-TV sport. Maybe it's something like a car crash. You know it involves real people and that something unexpected, maybe terrible, has just happened, so you can't tear your eyes away. Somehow Int-TV makes people feel more alive, more connected to each other, more something. It feels real. It feels like it matters. And the Int-TV version is designed to pull people in and keep them watching. Internet-Television needs viewers, as live set decoration, as emotional investors, as page clickers, and bandwidth hoggers. Nowadays Terra Ludus needs them too. The underlying economic structure has changed so much that Terra Ludus would struggle to survive without Int-TV, without sport tourism and wealthy fans, without the sponsors and advertisers who seduce people into caring enough to buy the subscriptions and merchandise that keep professional sports going.

Why shouldn't women's ball be part of that again? Globalizing and locating the former WNBA on Terra Ludus had worked for a while, until the men's league jettisoned it. Just because all the previous attempts to create a sustainable professional women's league had failed, surely that didn't mean it would this time.

But maybe she was getting ahead of herself. It was just a meeting. Maybe they were doing it just for show. It would all sound great. 'See how responsive we are to the public? We even brought this ex-ludio to NBB HQ at our own expense to talk with her.' And then, some weeks later, if they had to, they'd make a small announcement that they had looked at the options in detail but in the end it wasn't financially viable. And they didn't want to waste funding on something for a marginal audience segment. But, even if that was the likely outcome, there was no point going into the meeting thinking like a defeatist. And the head of programming was a woman so that might be a positive (or not, since some women Danny had interviewed at the top of male-dominated professions were even more anti-women than the men).

Stop it. I need to expel these thoughts. The vision of Simeon's I'm-an-idiot headshake appeared in her mind's eye. *Good idea. Do something physical to shift my state.* So she rotated her shoulders and rolled her head, side to side in rapid controlled movements. Tried to rattle those thoughts right off their tracks, and replace them with positivity. *Nothing ventured, nothing gained,* and all that.

And she started to write down names.

VID WORLD

She boarded the zoomer early, found a window seat, powered up (earbuds in) and started with her publicly accessible wor-mail. It showed 300 messages in the last day-night cycle. Simeon was right. The vid was generating interest. The subject lines were almost exclusively related to it. In two hours, she'd never get through them all. So she set the system to word-cloud all new messages and sipped a black coffee while it did its work. The wordle appeared on screen. Basketball was at the center. Not surprising. NBB was also prominent. Right and Best and Watch appeared nearby. So did Men and Girls. In slightly smaller type were Slower, Boring, Faster, Exciting.

Hmmm. A few binary oppositions there. And she was pretty sure which ones were attached to the women's game. There were some surprising terms though. Idiots, Pioneer, Equality, Subscription, Cancel, Support, Top, Best, Help, Awesome. Looked like there was some support out there.

She opened the vid on sportsfreak with a prickle of excitement and trepidation. The ticker showed more than 2,000 comments and the vid was the site's top bandwidth hogger. Wow. Nothing she'd done before had bandhogged to that extent. If nothing else she might get some freelance opportunities out of it. She immediately wordled the comments. Again the binary but this time it was mostly negative terms that dominated. Basketball and NBB again, but also Lesbos (looked like the 'femme' approach hadn't convinced everyone), Bitches, Slow, Boring, Public, Rights, Time, Now, Never. When she saw Second and Rate at about the same size she mentally put them together (and in smaller type saw Second-rate) so she had a good idea where that stream of argument was going. It looked like more than a hundred individual terms. But the wordle didn't really take her anywhere useful because it was words in combination (like Shut and Up) that would really give her insight into the tenor of the responses. So she set Psychia in motion. A friend sent her the app and she loves it. Designed last year by a psychiatrist to look for patterns in sentences, rather than single words, it cost a mint and hogged bandwidth like nobody's business but in Danny's line of work it had been an amazing tool for quickly sifting online data to get a taste of the public mood. While it worked in the background – it would take only half an hour if she was lucky – she sampled some of the comments. She didn't open any of the now-50 vid responses. She'd rather save her bandwidth for analysis.

Nglam7289 wished she would take her ideas, stuff them back in a basketball and drive a rotordam over it. Or stuff them in a pumpkin and feed them to an elephant.

I'm sure Psychia will have some fun with this one.

Terralien complimented her on her outfit and noted that the fact she had breasts meant her ideas were immediately suspect. Confidently, he pointed out that science had proven female hormones rendered women's thinking null and void at least one week per month and ventured that it might be that week in Danny's life. Then he wondered how Int-TV would be able to cope with the inevitable hormonal ups and downs in women's abilities to play basketball. 'Will it be adequate one week and appalling the next?' he asked. 'Will the coaches need larger rosters than the men so they can rest the athletes for those games they shouldn't be playing?' Then he questioned the fairness of women's teams being allowed more athletes than the men. Terralien signed off hoping Danny would post a more sensible vid next week retracting her clearly preposterous statements.

I thought this way of thinking had died out early-century but clearly the echoes of old ideas are still reverberating. Danny couldn't resist mentally creating the idea of a week off each month, luxuriating in a resort (soft mattresses, daily massages, long soaking baths and comfort food) all at the League's expense. Huh! Not likely. Women played through all kinds of pain. Perhaps that could be a marketing angle. Watch the women. They're so tough they play through any kind of pain. Even the kinds men will never know. The background could be a cartoon-like enormous splat of blood. The headline could be blood and guts. She giggled. That would turn people's heads. Talk about changing perspective.

Sportgirl92 told Terralien he was full of sh*t. And challenged him to a shoot out while she was 'in that week' to prove how wrong he was. She wrote, 'Girls can do anything and you better get used to it because I bet your boss is a woman. And I bet she doesn't take a week off every month'. And she told him his science was outdated disproven claptrap that only old sexists who hadn't mentally made it into this century were capable of thinking.

You go girl. But Danny was wary of the challenge to a shoot out option because there was always the danger that a loss could be used to 'prove' Terralien's truth.

Bizzman007 launched into an extended explanation of why women's sport couldn't be sold. Danny skipped most of it because she'd heard this argument so many times before. But somehow she would have to be prepared with answers to that hoary old resistance. She could use netball, a predominantly women's sport, as a good example. They'd gone from strength to strength in the last 50 years and now had a 10-nation league, a world championship every two years, and sponsors lining up to be involved. She'd get in touch with Laura Aurelion, CEO of Septum Pila, the International Netball Federation, and see what arguments they used. She might see women's basketball as competition but Danny would cross that bridge when she came to it. Better see what NBB was proposing first.

Over a 10-minute period as she scrolled through more comments, the words started to hammer at her. In comment after comment vitriol poured out: man-hater, ugly, lesbian, crap, wanker, women's sport is shit, no-one cares, Terra Ludus for men, women like you should be sterilized and shot, tiny mind, bitch, bitch, bitch.

A spurt of saliva filled her mouth, closely followed by a wave of nausea, as her gag reflex engaged. *All that venom, all that hate and anger. Where is it coming from? All I suggested was that women's sport deserved a fair share.* As she wondered how to deal with this, her body made the decision for her. She barely reached the bathroom, her stomach heaving as she resisted the upward flow, before a swirling, indeterminate, porridgey mass – *why does it always contain iridescent lumps of carrot* – erupted into the less-than-hygienic toilet bowl. She stayed on her knees for a few seconds, then rose slowly, leaned on the sink and rinsed the remnants from her mouth. Checked her clothes. Luckily her aim had been effective. *What just happened? What am I doing?*

When she returned to her seat, Psychia was done. And it wasn't a pretty picture. The emotions analysis was dominated by just two terms: Anger and Resentment. Attack and Challenge were also visible. Support and Counterchallenge were half the size. Looked like Terralien was in the vast majority. Given what had just happened, she knew that reading more negative comments could be dangerous, and she needed to be strong and positive for the meeting. So she clicked on Support. That was another great feature of Psychia. Not only did it organize by phrases and sentences but it was able to identify the underlying emotions and let you link directly to the responses it identified as representing those emotions.

Amoreludus immediately lifted her spirits. 'Daniela is right on,' the post started. 'And it's about time that someone had the courage to say it publicly. We're almost halfway through the 21st century, for Gaia's sake. This whole male-female thing is so passé. It's more than a hundred years since we learned that "Women can do anything". And they can. And that includes playing basketball. Who cares if most of them can't dunk. What is dunking anyway but some macho display of outdated masculinity? I don't care about that. But watching highly skilled strategy; that's what counts as sport for me. I'm ready to buy a subscription tomorrow. Listen up NBB. The future is now.'

chickzrool agreed and made the case that what little she was able to see of women's basketball suggested it was a better game than the men's. 'The guys are so individualistic. It's all about me, me, me. And it prigs me off when someone is wide open and the guy with the ball tries to go to the hoop on his own. Pass the prigging ball. Last year's women's world champs final was awesome. Like the vid said, I love the passing. It's awesome, trying to anticipate who's actually going to take the shot. It increases the tension, adds to the excitement. And we usually bet on how many passes it will take. It's pointless in a men's game. Men's ball could learn a lot from us women. So, yeah, NBB give us something new, something exciting, something different. Everyone should have the chance to see what a great game it is. Chickz rool, yeah!'

politicoma reminded NBB of its responsibilities. 'Grow a spine, NBB' it began. 'Ignore all the moaners and whiners and mad men. They get more than enough of what they want. Give the rest of us something we want – or that we could want if we had a chance to see enough to care about it. When I think about NBB sport, all I can hear is the words of that last century classic "It's raining men" running through my head. But there's no "Hallelujah" for me or my friends. Women are half the world. You've got a responsibility to show that half, and not just in the fashion section. So get on with it.'

Ludi-ball made the case that he personally didn't want to watch women's ball but he respected their right to be seen. 'Put them on,' he wrote. 'Maybe not in prime time but surely there's room for regular coverage. Don't cut the men's back but I'm sure you can squeeze it in somewhere. Cut back on those snooker competitions maybe (is that really sport?) And, anyway, they can stream and watch it anytime. I agree it's slower and less exciting but it's the best that women can manage so we (or they) should be able to see it.'

Talk about damning with faint praise. And clearly he didn't understand that most people don't bother to watch once the results are known. Still, Danny would take it. If some men were supportive that might help NBB 'grow a spine' and do something that would (apparently) be unpopular, at least initially.

matureballer12 was adamant women's basketball would be quality viewing. 'I play regularly with an ex-ludio and she kicks my ass and those of my other male friends,' he wrote. 'She can shoot the eyes out of the hoop. And none of us can stop her. And some of us were semi-pro back in the day. So I know women can play. They're smart too. Most of these bloggarts haven't even seen a women's game. What did the Romans say? Build it and they will come? So build the audience, put some effort and overheads into it and I think you'll be surprised. People hate change, but some change is good. And this is one of them.'

It was the use of bloggarts that gave Simeon away. It was one of his made up words – a mix of braggart and blogger – his favorite dismissive for those he thinks don't know anything. She was sure it was him, and it surprised her how much better she felt as she read the post. She decided to stop there, and review her key points for the meeting. The zoomer was already on the outskirts of Cupertino, skimming alongside established neighborhoods. It wouldn't slow down until it was closer in.

Five miles out, she linked to her parents. "Where are you?" said Dad peering at his screen.

"On my way to Mountain View, almost there. NBB contacted me this morning. They saw my vid and want to talk to me."

"Where? Talk about what? What vid?"

"The one I posted yesterday. About starting a women's league. I sent you a link. Didn't you see it?"

"Sorry. Not yet. I've been busy in the garden. Gearing up for spring planting."

She's not really surprised. Her parents are old school, still live in the rurality, about two hours away from her, and their apple and berry farm with its rambling wildflower and vege gardens became their 'baby' once she left home.

"How's it going?" Knowing this was the right question.

"Oh. You know. Pruning the trees, ordering strawberry plants and extra fertilizer. The weeds have taken off early this year. All that unseasonable rain I suppose."

The zoomer was slowing and the electronic signboard showed 90 seconds to the station.

"Sorry Dad, gotta go. I'm nearly at the station."

"Good luck I guess. You'll do well. You always do," he said. "Ping us tonight and let us know how it went."

THE MEETING

As promised, the Escort was there. Silent, as they usually were, holding an electronic sign with her name on it. She nodded, scanned her ID and followed him towards the East exit. He turned abruptly left, down two blocks and gestured her towards a revolving glass door, clearly new but made to look like early 21st century engineering. Scanning up the front of the building (200 storeys she thought she remembered reading somewhere), she caught a glimpse of the famous blinking NBB neon sign. Now that was seriously old school. Neon went out of fashion at least 30 years ago, before she was born, once they perfected algal phosphorescent lighting. Free, organic, produced by algae and bugs.

A frisson of excitement rippled through her. She was really here. After entering she turned to thank the Escort but he had already disappeared. As she approached the main desk, Imelda Consonati exited the quickriser, and waved the security guard aside.

"Welcome," she said. "So nice to meet you in person."

"Thank you. The pleasure is mine." And it was true. She was happy to be here, and the nerves had disappeared just as they did once she stepped onto the court and the whistle blew. She wondered what to call the NBB programming head. Imelda seemed a little informal but Ms Consonati was even worse. She'd just have to avoid it altogether.

"Follow me Daniela. May I call you Daniela?" Danny nodded. "Lovely. And you can call me Imelda." *Oh well, one problem solved.* The quickriser was almost silent, paneled with some kind of vintage wood, recycled California redwood perhaps. Another tip of the hat to last century. A way, she supposed, of making it clear that NBB had history, heft, prominence. She barely felt her stomach drop as they sped towards the 198th floor.

"Who will we be meeting with?" she asked, hoping the use of we wasn't too presumptuous.

"Initially, just me. Then I'll bring in the NBB CEO. If we make progress, we'll discuss some options with the NBB Board, who are meeting later today to agree the annual programming line-up. That's why I was keen to get you here."

Prig. This sounded much more serious, much more formal than she'd expected. Good thing she'd dressed up. Suddenly her bladder demanded attention. She really needed to pee. She'd meant to take care of it at the station – she couldn't face going back into the zoomer bathroom – but the Escort had been waiting. As the riser doors opened, she asked for directions to the nearest facility.

"Don't worry," said Imelda. "You can use mine."

The only word to describe Imelda's office was … actually there wasn't a word. Danny stood at the entrance trying not to gape at the 180-degree view of Mountain View and the ocean, the other citie-scrapers stacked like Lego-blocks well below them. Imelda smiled.

"Not bad huh? One of the perks of the job. And quite necessary given the hours. The bathroom's over there," pointing to an inconspicuous door set into the 8-foot high timber-lined wall. In the bathroom, Danny tried to center herself, taking 10 slow deep breaths, looking inwards and reminding herself that they had come to her. And it sounded like this was something more than a placate-the-public exercise. There was another door and she peeked through it into a tiny but fully equipped sleeping space comprising an immaculately made king-sized bed, side table and bedside lamp, with a tiny round window that would give a view of the ocean when the bed's occupant was sitting up. Not bad indeed, although it didn't look like it got a lot of use. Not a single personal item was on display. It was as spartan and impersonal as a hotel room.

When she returned, Imelda was seated at a round business table, with an icom in front of her projecting onto the back wall. Danny was surprised to see her Canestri Mulier profile, her current work Int-site and a freeze-frame of the vid jostling for attention. She sat.

"Right. Let's get to it." Imelda clearly didn't have time to waste. "I saw your vid. I liked it. I've been trying to get the Board to see that we need to expand our sports audience and I think your proposal is the best one to cross my desk. It helps that you're good-looking because we'll need that on screen. We can work on your hairstyle and make up."

"Could you slow down a bit?" Danny managed to interject as her mind tried to process what was happening. "What do you mean on screen? And why should it matter what I look like?"

Imelda just raised her eyebrows. "Surely that's why you posted the vid," she said. "You're looking for an on-screen role. And I think you'd be right for it. You've got the journalism background, the basketball pedigree and knowledge. And we need someone to front the promotion of the new league until it gets underway. I just needed to meet you in person to be sure."

"Wait a minute." Things were moving way too fast. "That's not why I did it. And I'm not looking to be on Int-TV. I like my job."

"I don't know how you survive on that income," Imelda continued, undeterred. "We know how much you earned the last two years. We'll triple it and build in bonuses linked to clicks and bandwidth hog time."

"But…" Danny paused, not sure if she was furious (*how dare they find that kind of background information on me?*) or intrigued (*it might be fun to be on-screen, and the guys would have a fit*). "It's not what I came here for," she found herself saying. "Does this mean you're possibly seriously considering broadcasting women's ball?"

"There's no possibly involved," came the rapid reply. "Of course we're serious. Why else would we bother bringing you here? I want to strike now, while your vid is generating clicks, while the Board is vulnerable to persuasion. They abhor bad publicity just slightly more than they resist change and this is a change I've long felt would take us in the right direction. So. Are you in?"

Danny blew out a deep breath and shrugged her shoulders. "Why not, I guess."

"Good. You're the key because you're the one with the current public profile."

"But I don't have a public profile," Danny protested.

"Really? Have you checked the Int stats today?" Imelda's fingers flew across the virtual keyboard, pulling up the daily Int data.

Danny's vid was in the top 10 trending stories. It already had 2 million views.

"It won't be long before news media will be after you," Imelda continued. "Haven't you had any pings yet?

"I was running a hog program," Danny replied, "so I don't think anyone could get through. Then I turned off my icom for this meeting."

"Well don't turn it on yet. If the Board agrees, and you agree to terms, we'll handle the publicity and announcements."

Imelda had the style of a drill sergeant. It felt like echoes of Terra Ludus when the coach controlled every aspect of her life. She hadn't liked it then and she wasn't sure she liked it now. Imelda was already vidding with the CEO. She brought him up on screen.

"David Ailao, Daniela Bartoli. Daniela, David." Danny gave the non-verbal Terra Ludan upward chin lift of acknowledgement, David responded with the standard Terra Altrix downward nod.

"Right. David. Time is short and Daniela has agreed to be our face of the new league. So I think we can get this project before the Board. Do you have the material I just sent?" Danny was somewhat relieved to see the CEO being subjected to the same drill sergeant interaction.

"Yes thanks," said David. "I'll have it before them in 10 minutes. I've been doing some priming and I think they're ready to agree. Sandy's working on the announcement and Chandra's been doing further liaison with the teams. Ten are on board in principle and four more are discussing it with their management teams but the initial signs are positive."

"Great. I'll go over terms with Daniela and we'll wait to hear from you. Good hunting." And Imelda sliced out.

"Wow. This is amazing. I only just posted the vid and you've got all this organized already?" It was a mix of statement and question.

"Actually, we've been doing background work on it for a while but the time was never quite right. Now it is. Thanks to you." Imelda's conspiratorial smile transformed her face. *Nothing like my old coaches.* "And it makes us look good to be responding to public demand rather than introducing something that is initially going to be unpopular."

"So you have read some of the responses."

"Of course. We're not going into this blind. And you shouldn't either. Once you sign up for this, you've got be prepared. You'll be loved and hated. And in the beginning, hate will be the most visible and the most public. The macho-minds aren't going to like this."

Danny nodded vigorously. "I know a few who will have a fit," she said. "And they're my friends!" She laughed. "They are going to have a cow if I do this."

"I like your attitude," Imelda shot back. "But they'll come around or get over it. People hate change and basketball's tied to all that stupid (money-making but stupid) outdated gender rubbish, so there'll be a rocky start I predict."

"So why are you doing it?" Danny didn't want to get into this just to become male public enemy number one.

"Because we have to. Our subscriptions are falling, and we're losing female audiences at a greater rate. Our market research is pretty clear that women, and quite a lot of men, are interested in women's basketball and are likely to buy subscriptions. We'll lose some men at the beginning but I think we can build the audience and present a product that will bring them back."

"So what's in it for me, other than a lot of abuse? I've seen enough of that already today."

"A damn fine income, for one. And a commitment from me that NBB is in this for the long haul. We're making a five-year commitment to broadcast women's games, in a six-month season. Right now we're thinking 14 teams, playing each other twice, with a pre-season, quarter and semi-finals series and the finals. We'll provide a dedicated league Int-site, support for individual team sites, including technological expertise in vlogging and vid-making, and Tier 1 bandwidth on Terra Ludus so all the teams have quality access."

Danny wasn't sure whether this was a dream or reality. She actually pinched herself hard, on her left thigh, invisible under the table, just to be sure.

"Yes it's real," Imelda said, clearly reading her facial expressions (hopefully she wasn't a mind reader or hadn't hidden a micro-eye under the table).

"So. Are you in? Here's the contract. On paper only. We don't circulate them. I have an independent lawyer on standby to talk you though it or we'll pay a lawyer in Los Angeles as long as you can organize it by tomorrow. We really need an answer quickly because I need to get the publicity machine underway." Imelda's voice quietened. "Assuming David gets the job done of course."

Right now, Danny understood what it must have been like to ride a real roller coaster. She didn't know if she was up or down. Dropping or flying. Things were upside down and sideways, all at the same time. She'd come here expecting to have to make her case, to a skeptical and possibly condescending audience. Now her notes and thoughts lay discarded. She was, in short, way out of her depth but hope was stirring, and with it so were equal shares of fear and excitement. The face of the women's league. Could she do it? Why not? Maybe she could even do commentary once the league started. She knew the game inside out, and still had contacts with some of the key coaches. And she'd be criticized no matter what. None of the male play-by-play commentators would know the women's game as well as the women professional athletes or coaches.

"The commentary team," she said. "They'll all be women won't they? People who know the women's game? Who appreciate its subtleties?"

"I can't guarantee that." Imelda gave it to her straight. "That's what I want to see but it will depend on you and the other possible ex-players and coaches who apply for the roles. If we can find the right mixes from within the game I'll back you. If we can't then we'll have to move some of our men over, probably in play-by-play roles."

Danny's heart sank. She knew those commentators, had listened to them for years. Most of them didn't even acknowledge that women played the sport, and some were outright derisory. It could be a disaster.

"So what role do you see me in? Play-by-play or expert? Sideline? Studio anchor?" She realized she had automatically assumed she would do play-by-play. A bit presumptive perhaps.

"I don't know yet. We'll have to try you out to see where your skills are. At the start you'll be our 'face', fronting the advertising

campaign, doing appearances, interviews, talk shows, all the usual."
The flow stopped as Danny felt Imelda pausing to really look at her.

"Sorry," she said. "I'm rushing ahead as I usually do. What do
you think you'd like to do?"

"I don't know," was Danny's first response but it wasn't what
she really wanted to say. But she was here, wasn't she? She'd made the
vid because she didn't want to sit back. And she really knew the game.
"Actually I do know," she said. "I'd like to try play-by-play. Or maybe
the expert commentator role. I know how women's basketball should
be presented. I know what's unique and special about it. And I don't
want some men's basketball commentator doing it wrong, comparing
it to the men's, demeaning it." That was more words than Danny had
spoken since she arrived but when she looked up Imelda was nodding.

"That's the spirit. That's the passion I saw in the vid. That's
what we need to anchor the way we present it. Play-by-play might not
be the best place to achieve that, but I'm open. I know you haven't
worked in broadcast Int before but those interviews you did last year
for the vid on Mars terrascaping showed you have natural talent and
the screen likes you. So there are a number of ways you could go.
But the first six months will be promotion while we get the league
organized, train the coaches and athletes, along with a dedicated team
of commentators, producers, cam-ops and directors to do it our way.
Can you do that? It will mean a fair bit of travelling and networking
and some Int and vid appearances. Do you have any commitments that
you can't get out of?"

As Danny mentally checked through her work flow, she
realized she had already been enticed (railroaded?) into taking the job.
She wanted it. This was a chance to make history. How could she turn
it down? And a regular salary wouldn't go astray.

"Not really," she said. "I have one major feature I need to
finish up that involves some travel but maybe I could combine those
interviews with basketball activities." She caught Imelda's smirk of
success out of the corner of her eye. Oh well, did it really matter that
she'd implicitly agreed to do it? So she turned and grinned directly
back at her. "I have a cat who will need to be cared for while I'm away.
And I try to visit my parents at least every second Sunday. Saturdays

I play pick up and watch the men's league with four friends. We each take turns hosting on game-day. I did it last week so I'm off the hook for the next month. Fridays I usually meet my best friends for dinner. The rest of the time I chase freelance stories. That's my life. So, yes, I think I can do it. And I'm willing to talk to your independent lawyer."

Danny picked up the contract as the vid pinged. David's face filled the screen. He didn't need to say anything. Danny jerked in her seat as Imelda pounded the table hard, just once, in celebration.

"They went for it," David said. "The vote was 15–4. The league starts in six months and they signed off on all our terms: 5 year commitment, 14 teams, everything." He virtually high-fived Imelda and she fived him back. "I'll be in touch again in two hours. The team is on it." He raised his eyebrows questioning. Imelda nodded. "Welcome to the team, Daniela," he said. "Good to have you on board. Look forward to meeting you soon." And the screen went blank.

"Where is he?" Danny had assumed the Board meeting was somewhere nearby.

"Terra Ludus. The Board likes to meet somewhere interesting and most of them are basketball fans so we had already organized for them to tour the Basketball Hall of Fame. David was there to lead the tour and subtly reinforce the invisibility of women's basketball. Looks like it worked."

Danny agreed about the invisibility. The women's section, such that it was, was tiny. The information was sparse, the vids low quality – some so bad that the Hall of Fame refused to play them on the big screen at the entrance.

"Can you delay your return?" Imelda's question drew Danny back into the present. "We can put you up overnight and zoom you back tomorrow. I'd like you to have a chance to discuss things with the lawyer, and meet the team. And I can give you privacy and bandwidth to contact your family, arrange care for the cat, talk to whomever you need to reach. Will that work?"

Danny nodded. She was impressed by the reference to her cat. Bumbles didn't like to be home alone for long periods, even though he could get outside at will, down the cat-friendly 'ladder' her dad constructed and attached to the window of her second-floor bedroom.

Who could feed him? Nancy was on vacation and Vicky was working in a hinterland hospital for the week. Mom and Dad were getting ready for spring planting and it was too far. Perhaps Marley Dean next door could do it, and she knew where Danny kept the spare key.

"Got your icom?" Imelda's voice interrupted her thoughts. "While you're in this room it's free. I've got to talk to a few people and arrange for the lawyer, so you've got 15 minutes. Is that enough?"

"Should be. Thanks."

Imelda strode towards the door, tossing a final comment over her shoulder. "And remember, don't respond to any media."

Another nod. Danny woke her icom. Twenty-six messages. They would have to wait. She pinged Simeon, who responded immediately.

"Hey there," she began. "Guess what?"

"You've found a boyfriend in Mountain View. That was fast work." His familiar sarcasm was just what she needed. Then she realized she didn't know if she was allowed to say anything. Nothing was official yet.

"Look. I can't talk for long but something really amazing is going to happen." She couldn't help beaming. Simeon's expression turned alert, thoughtful. "I don't think I can say anything else but you know why I came down here. I'm staying overnight but I'll be back tomorrow."

He raised his eyebrows. She raised hers back. He gave her a thumbs-up. She gave him a double one back. He silently mouthed 'wow' and she mouthed 'double wow'. She wasn't sure why they weren't talking but it felt right not to say anything aloud. His lips formed the word 'really?' She nodded, and nodded, and nodded, and nodded, faster and faster. She really wanted to jump up and dance around the room but that didn't feel appropriate in this sound-absorbing luxury.

"What about Bumbles? Who's feeding him?"

"I was going to ask Marley, my next-door neighbor. She's almost always around."

"I can do it if you like. Bumbles knows me a bit. Just tell me where the spare key and food are."

"That's really kind but you don't have to do that."

41

"It's no problem really. I have to be over your side of town this afternoon so I'll drop in on my way home.

"Are you sure?"

"Of course. You ever hear me volunteer for something I didn't want to do? Now where are the key and food?"

"Key is inside the tag on the doormat. And, no, it's not easy to find. The inside of the tag is magnetized and the key is light. Bend down and take your shoes off at the door so no-one sees you picking it up. Cat food's in the fridge (the code is 3X10). Spare tins are in the top right side of the bi-fold cupboard. He gets 1 tin, fresh water, and refresh his bowl of dry food. Can you hang around for five minutes and run the tap in the bath for him after he's eaten? You've seen him do that. Don't ask me where it came from, but he loves to drink running water."

"Got it. You've probably got some other calls to make." She nodded. "So I'll go. Let me know when you can tell me more or I'll see you at my place Saturday." She waved as he sliced out.

By nineteenth hour, she had spoken with her parents – worried about the travel but happy to hear about the steady income. "Don't accept the first offer. They always leave a bit in reserve." That was her mother. "If the salary is set, see if you can get more holidays, or a bigger bonus."

"Thanks Mom. Will do." At least she had some experience negotiating contracts although it sounded like this was in a whole new realm.

Then she reached Vic who validated her decision to go for it. "Looking forward to hanging out with a celebrity. Don't forget us when you're being courted by all the vogues."

"Never going to happen. Anyway, I'll need someone to keep my feet on the ground, what with all the fawning and voguish parties!"

A quiet knock on the door preceded the entry of a young man. How did she know he was the lawyer? The subtly tailored suit, crisp white shirt, and understated tie were sure reveals. He was carrying nothing but a rose-colored icom, coordinated with the hint of pink in his tie. Dark hair, stylish cut, deep brown eyes, gleaming olive skin and an inviting smile. Totally swoonable, as Vic would say. Of course Int-TV was full of beautiful people. *What the hell am I doing here?*

"Hey Vic. I've got to go. The lawyer's here." She switched the vid view and heard Vic's gasp, followed by a giggle. "Right. Enjoy (heavy emphasis) your meeting. Talk to you soon. Over and out."

"Daniela Bartoli?"

"Yes. Come in. You must be the lawyer."

"Santos Oliviera at your service." He introduced himself with a stylish mock bow, Spanish-style. "And I mean that. I am completely independent of NBB. My job is to explain the contract and give you advice about what you may be agreeing to. May I join you?"

And the negotiations began. The contract was surprisingly straightforward. One year guaranteed salary (and at the promised three times what she made last year), with an option to extend for up to four more. In year one, she would earn a 10% bonus for every 100,000 new subscribers, and a salary increase in the extended years if subscriptions continued to grow. Starting date next Monday.

"Are you sure that one year is enough?" Santos raised the first question. "That's not very secure and Int-TV is a tough business. You could be unemployed in just 12 months."

"It's no problem for me," she said. "I'm a freelance journalist. Just knowing how much is coming in each month will be a new experience. And I don't want to be in Int-TV. I'm only doing it for the principle. Although, actually, it's beginning to sound quite exciting."

Scrutinizing her moisturized and lipsticked but otherwise cosmetic-free face, he continued. "Then the only other question I have is how do you feel about the dress code clause?" At her shrug of unconcern, he continued. "What it means is that they can tell you what clothes to wear – they'll provide them – how to style your hair and prescribe cosmetics. Different ones for day and night, on-screen or public appearances. You'll have to learn how to do it yourself."

She shrugged her shoulders again. "Whatever it takes, I guess."

"No. Really," he said. "This will be a big change. You'll have a public image to maintain. I saw your vid by the way. Very impassioned. And you looked good – natural and warm. That's why they want you."

To have a gorgeous man say such things was making her feel pretty damn good. She didn't usually worry about her looks but the flattery was not unpleasant at all. Then he continued.

"But that won't stop them trying to turn you into a pretty puppet. They're likely to insist that you have Botox and possibly cosmetic surgery." Danny jerked in shock. *Botox. Cosmetic surgery. But that's crazy.*

"I'd resist it if I were you. I could try to moderate the clause if you like. Something like the wardrobe has to be negotiated between you, and that you'll wear the make-up styles they prescribe when on-screen or at official functions but otherwise you control how you look. You also control what happens to your body, including around cosmetic enhancements. What do you think?"

It sounded fine to her, better than fine. And she thought about playing pick-up with the guys. There's no way she'd be wearing make-up for that kind of activity. Or on a run. Nor could she imagine having surgery or Botox. This was a job, a one-year gig most likely. It shouldn't rule her life.

"Thanks. I'd like that. I don't really like wearing make-up. In fact I consciously made an effort for the vid. So I don't want to go much further than that if I don't have to."

"You'll have to," he said. "But I'll rewrite the clause to limit its reach. OK?"

After she agreed to the changes, Santos disappeared to meet with the NBB lawyer. She didn't have the energy to worry about what happened next. She closed her eyes and leaned back in the chair. Gaia she was exhausted. It felt like a swarm of bumblebees was holding a convention in her brain. It was hard to think for all the noise in there. Everything was happening so fast.

She awoke with a start, a painful backward head jerk bringing her back to the present. She stretched her neck, rotated her shoulders backwards and up and down. Stood up, circled each arm forward and backward 10 times. Limbering up. Getting ready for the next phase.

Imelda strode back in, two copies of the revised contract in one hand and two boxes in the other. "We can live with this," she said, placing the boxes on the table and handing Danny one copy of the contract. "As long as you're willing to meet with our makeup people and learn some basic skills for everyday use. Are you ready to sign? Can you be back here next Tuesday? We can put you in an NBB serviced apartment to start with. You'll need to be available 24-hours a day for the first couple of weeks. You'll spend Tuesday and Wednesday training, and we'll make the League announcement at the end of the week. I'll send you some materials to read. In the meantime, I recommend you finish up any other jobs, survey the Int and make your own summary of what people are saying, identifying the general feelings for and against. Come on Tuesday with ideas about how to counter or further support the major ones. Use your journalism skills. We'll have our own people on it, but I want to see what you come up with as well. You're a basketballer so you'll be better placed to sift."

"In for a penny, in for a pound." She couldn't shake off the old sayings. Whenever she didn't know what to say, Dad's words just flowed out of her. Sometimes she got odd looks, but she couldn't help it. The words were etched into her DNA, family echoes that she valued and saw no reason to give up.

Imelda pushed the boxes across the table to her. "Pick one," she instructed. "These are the latest NBB flexismart data bracelets."

While Imelda continued explaining the bracelet's features, Danny lifted one lid to find a two-inch wide silver-colored band with intricate side patterns reminiscent of the Terra Ludus koru design and a subtly glowing timeclock on the outer surface. *I don't really care what it can do. I love it. This is so cool.*

"You'll need one for all your NBB travel and accommodation," Imelda explained. "It will hold all your electronic data, including tickets, travel and accommodation bookings and salary. It has the standard skin projection so you can work in any conditions, and it is water- and sweat-proof. On your way out, the IT manager will set up your two-step authentication. He's waiting at the front desk. We'll bracket it with your icom next week. For now, it only holds your train and taxi tickets. You know how they work? A quick flick of the wrist turns the projection on and off."

Danny nodded her understanding. She had tried one a few years earlier as part of a story on the latest tech gizmos but at the time it was out of her price range.

"The other one is in gold, different pattern. Which do you want?"

Danny opened the other box to be polite but she'd already made her choice.

"Silver please," she said, picking it up, and trying to act like receiving a top-of-the-line device was an everyday occurrence. It slid easily over her wrist, subtly tightening to a close-fitting grip, ensuring it would not come off easily. With an experimental wrist flick, an oblong of light appeared on her inside arm, the NBB logo glowing in its center. She flicked it off again. Then she remembered the one question she needed to ask. "What can I tell my family and friends? Can I tell them about the new league?"

Imelda shook her head. "Not until we make the announcement next week."

"So how do I explain my new role?"

"You can't. That was in the small print. You can't tell anyone about the job until we announce it publicly. I suggest you explain that we liked some of your ideas and have invited you down next week to talk through them in more detail."

"But my family will be really upset when they hear the announcement on Int or vid news rather than from me."

Imelda paused to consider her point. The smallest of frowns appeared. Danny continued, "And I've already told my parents and best friend about the job offer."

"Well. That's that cat out of the bag. What you can say is that you've been given a short-term contract to help develop news about women's basketball. But you must keep the league news confidential. Can you do that?"

Danny nodded as Imelda stood up (Danny followed suit) and shook Danny's hand formally.

"Welcome to the NBB team. I'm sure you're anxious to get some sleep. We've booked you into Abode just round the corner. Breakfast is provided. An Escort is waiting. And another will meet you at sixth-hour-and-20 tomorrow. You're on the seventh hour zoomer. Don't forget to set up your bracelet on your way out."

Imelda was heading towards the door, clearly indicating with a sweep of her arm that Danny was to follow.

"See you next week." Danny's words were no sooner out of her mouth than Imelda had disappeared back into her office, the door automatically closing behind her. *That was fast. Guess that puts me back in my place.* Danny caught the lifter to reception and happily submitted to the 10-minute authentication process, involving a scan of both forefingers and little fingers and her left and right irises. She selected a four-digit initial password, which served as the first-level authentication, to be followed by her choice of the biometric measures. After several tests to ensure the authentication worked and her tickets were properly loaded, she followed the Escort silently back to the hotel. She sent a group text to her parents, Nancy and Vic and Simeon. "All good. Home tomorrow. Talk then." Planning to take a shower, she made the mistake of lying down on the bed first. She was asleep within minutes, sinking down into unknowingness, the bumblebees finally quiet.

On the zoomer home, she realized part of her salary would have to go towards care for Bumbles. There was no point moving him if she would be travelling. And she couldn't ask Nancy or Vic to move into her place long-term. Her friends could probably cover for the first week but she'd have to get something sorted quickly.

She silenced the vid, set the phone to give her five minutes warning before Union Station and tuned in some ambient sounds. She needed soothing tranquility, wordlessness if possible. She'd talk to everyone once she got home.

BACK TO NORMALITY?

Danny unlocked the front door into a warm apartment, the familiar scent of strawberry-mango tea filling the space. No sign of Bumbles. Dropping her bag just inside the door and removing her shoes, she rounded the screen that gave her living room some privacy from the entrance. Bumbles, ensconced on the couch on Simeon's lap, opened one eye and promptly went back to sleep. She stared. The sheepish grin on Simeon's face said it all.

"Couldn't get up," he said. "I'm cat-impaired."

"And you're drinking my tea," she responded.

Another sheepish grin. "Well, it's all you had in the cupboard except for that awful chai eggnog stuff, and it's actually quite tasty." At her smirk, he continued. "Just don't tell the guys, OK?"

"I could never rat out someone who took care of my cat."

"The kettle boiled a little while ago. Want to join us?"

A minute later, cup of tea in hand, she headed to the window seat, stopping to stroke Bumbles on the way past. He was purring, she realized. Not loudly as he usually started out but an almost subterranean vibration of pure contentment.

Settled with her legs stretched out along the length of the seat, she assessed Simeon and the cat. "Are you a secret cat whisperer? I've never seen Bumbles this relaxed with anyone except me."

"Not that I know of." She noted that his hand, seemingly unconsciously, was rhythmically stoking Bumbles' back. "I haven't had much to do with cats since I was a kid. But he seems to like me. I think he was missing you because he leapt onto me as soon as he'd eaten last night and I didn't have the heart to move him. Next thing I knew it was third hour this morning."

She laughed. "Yeah. I know. Did he give you that look? The semi-wounded one that seems to say, 'surely you aren't planning to go anywhere. I've just gotten comfortable?' I don't know why, but I find it really difficult to turf him off when he pulls that one."

"You got it," he said. "And I'd had a long day at work so I was a goner I think. Hope you don't mind but I borrowed one of your pillows and a blanket and spent the rest of the night on the couch. Bumbles was sleeping on my chest when I woke up an hour ago. So I grabbed a shower, and some breakfast and thought I'd wait 'til you got home."

His hair was wet, she saw, and his expression open, just checking she didn't mind him staying the night. And she didn't, she realized. She didn't know exactly what it was but his energy felt mellow and free somehow. Different. No façade. No shutters. Like somehow he was comfortable here. Something the cat seemed to have intuited.

"No problem. You didn't need to sleep on the couch though. You could have slept in the bed." She stopped talking, a vision of him in her bed startlingly real. An unexpected warmth suffused her cheeks. Gaia. What if Simeon saw? Trying to banish the image, she turned to look out the window with its peek of the ocean, wondering how long she had been silent and what she should say next.

"Earth to Danny. What's up with you?"

"What? Oh nothing. Just a bit brain-lagged. It was a really intense day yesterday. I'm still reeling."

"So what can you tell me?" She appreciated that he seemed to understand this was something big that she might not be able to share.

She took a deep breath and blew it out. Turned back. And beamed at him. "Depends how good you are at keeping secrets." She really wanted to tell him.

"Take it to the grave," he joked.

"No. Seriously. You really have to promise."

"Right. Hand over heart. I promise not to tell a solitary soul, or discuss it with anyone except Bumbles. Right Bumbles? You can keep a secret can't you?" He was still stroking Bumbles who deigned to open one eye to acknowledge his name. "See? We're in agreement, your cat and I."

"Alright. This is not the whole story," she prefaced it, "but this is what I can tell you. They've put me on a short-term contract to develop stories about women's basketball. They're going to train me ... "She got no further before Simeon leapt up to high five her. Bumbles simultaneously demonstrated his displeasure at being unceremoniously dumped on the couch, with claws and a loud meow.

Simeon's "Fantastic," was quickly followed by "Hey! That hurt." He rubbed his left thigh and gave Bumbles a piercing stare before turning back to Danny. "And ..."

"And they're going to train me to do on-air with a view to something more long-term. But that's all I'm allowed to say right now."

Simeon sat down again. Bumbles vacated the couch and stalked into the kitchen. "So, if you can't say anything more, can you answer some questions?"

"Maybe. Depends."

"When might you be able to tell me something more?"

Could she answer this? Perhaps. "Maybe the end of next week," she said.

"So that means something is going to be announced." Simeon was almost talking to himself. "Will there be an announcement by NBB late next week?"

"Probably." She was enjoying the challenge of revealing but not revealing. The game of it. The playful way he was approaching trying to find out more.

"Will it be something big?"

"Could be."

"Does it have something to do with your vid?"

"You already know the answer to that." She'd always thought he was smart. This conversation was confirming it.

"So," he mused further, leaning forward, taking up Rodin's The Thinker pose. Right elbow on right knee, forehead resting on his right fist. And very slowly, in a fake news announcer voice, staring at the ground, he continued. "Here's what we know. Something next week. Something big. Daniela Bartoli is on a 'short term' (emphasis) contract but they're training her for something on air. What could that mean?"

She knew he didn't expect an answer.

He continued, relinquishing the pose and leaning back on the couch, switching to a sports commentator patter and pacing. "So, ladies and gentlemen, it is my considered opinion that women's basketball's profile is about go interstellar and our guest Daniela Bartoli is going to be at the heart of it." Switching back to his normal voice, he acknowledged her with a firm nod. "This is so cool." She knew the excitement was writ large across her face. She couldn't hide it. But she didn't nod back. He knew enough.

"I have 'homework' this week," she said. "But I'm not sure I can do it alone. I've got to go through and summarize all the public responses to the vid, on those blogs and vlogs you found, and on my wor-mails. Imelda said its up to 2 million views, so who knows how many comments there are."

"5,400," came the immediate response. "As of eighth hour. And it's Imelda is it? I assume you're talking about Imelda Consonati, NBB's head of programming?"

"How do you know that?"

"I read. I research. I am all-knowing. And I now have an additional piece of information to consider. You on first name basis with the most powerful woman in Terra Altrix sports broadcasting. And rumor has it, she wants change because NBB's sport subscriptions are dropping." He cocked his head and turned a quizzical gaze on her.

"You're just like Bumbles when he catches a mouse," she said. "You want external validation that you're a clever clogs. Well I'm not giving it. You just keep thinking your deep thoughts until next week."

Faking a serious look, belied by the twinkle in his sparkling green eyes, he accepted her terms. "Deep thoughts it is. That's my diet for the next 10 days."

"Well maybe I can give you some sustenance, some food for thought, so to speak. I really do need some help going through the comments. They want me to figure out the main ways that people are reacting to my vid. Or at least how they're publicly reacting. And to come up with some ideas about how to challenge or build on them.

Do you have any time this weekend? I've got to submit my report by Tuesday and …" She paused, wondering whether to tell him about her visceral reaction to the small selection of comments she'd read. No. Definitely not. He'd think she was a flake. And should she tell him she thought he'd posted one in support? No again. Maybe she'd highlight that one in her analysis and see how he reacted.

"And you don't want to face all those bullshit comments by yourself. Right?"

"Right. I read some on the way up to Mountain View and it was a bit rough," she admitted. "To be honest, I've avoided looking at them since."

"How about coming over to my place about tenth hour on Saturday? Bring your icom. Then we'd have four hours before the game. I'm hosting it this week remember." She wondered how it would be to watch the games with the guys. Nothing like last week. The world felt like a new place, a foreign territory, frightening and exciting at exactly the same time. Excitening? Frixciting? Whatever. She'd just have to act normal. Whatever that was. Then again, they'd probably not even notice! So it really would be a piece of normality. Probably just what she needed.

"That would be great. I'll bring nachos as well. Should have time to make them Friday night. Can I bring Manu if he's still in town?"

"Sure. No problem. Simeon paused. "How come you told him about us, but we didn't know about him?"

"I don't know," she shrugged. "It just never came up I guess. I only talk to him a couple of times year. Usually I'm in touch with his sister, Moana, who I used to play with. But she's doing the Mommy-thing. Popping out grandkids, keeping the generations going. My parents stay in contact with Manu's mother and her generation. I guess that's how he found out where I live."

"Is he mah-or-ree? Did I say that right?" At her affirmative nod and repetition, "Māori," he continued. "And what did he mean when he said you have a bit of brown in you? I've never heard that term before."

She hesitated, wondering whether to give him her usual line about there being some Spanish in her background, hence the olive skin so prevalent in her family. But what she'd learned from hanging out with Manu's whānau was the importance of being proud of who you are, so she took the step into the unknown.

"Well," she began, "we tell the story that we're descendants of sailors from the Spanish Armada wrecked on the shores of Ireland in the 1500s. That line produced what's called the Black Irish, and that part is true. But it's not the whole story. My grandmother did some DNA testing of her parents and we're pretty sure there's a Native American ancestor somewhere. Hence the 'brown' which is kind of slang for Native or Indigenous. We don't know the tribe and there's no formal records, but my first ancestors emigrated here in the 1800s and spent a lot of time around native people. My gran did some genealogical research and found out that a couple of the women taught on reservations. And one of my…" – she counted off on her fingers – "great-great-great grandmothers I think, got married to a white guy and had a kid not long after.

"Have you ever tried to find out more? That would be cool."

"Not really. And while my grandmother's generation is still alive, none of us will. She thought it was worth exploring further, but it was a sensitive topic for her parents and some of the older people. They saw it as something best left in the past. So she told me and then put it aside."

"Yeah." He nodded. "My grandparents didn't want to talk much about the past either. It's a pity."

"Yes it is. But it helped me on TL. Although we were all welcomed onto the local marae – that's kind of like their village or family meeting place – I was the only one who got whāngai-ed. Apparently it's pretty rare. They took in my parents too and they always spent time at Manu's marae on the few times they could afford to visit me."

"That's cool. In fact, it's really cool. It connects you to both places. You're lucky. I don't have that."

"What do you mean? Your family's been here forever."

"Not really. My parents were the first generation born here. But they're still seen as Lebanese immigrants. Some people still ask me where I'm from, even though I have don't have an accent and I can barely speak a word of Arabic.

"That's so stupid. You're Altrixian just like the rest of us. We're a great big mixed salad. Us, and most of the rest of the world. Anyway, you speak a whole lot of languages don't you?"

"Yeah, but not my family's home language, although I can usually get by with French. I think I resisted it because I wanted to fit in. But it didn't really work." A long sigh escaped. "Oh well. Prig the lot of them. In the end, it doesn't matter. The people who know me, the companies that employ me, they don't care."

"And nor do I," she agreed, glancing down at her new bracelet timeclock. Nearly ninth hour. "Oh. Shouldn't you be at work?"

He checked his own. "Yeah. It's OK since I worked late yesterday but I better head out." He stood and headed to the door. "See you Bumbles. Thanks for the cuddles." Bumbles refused to appear. "I'll see you Saturday morning."

He reached out to give her a hug. She hesitated. They'd never hugged before. Punched each other on the arm, high-fived, all the usual celebratory actions on the court or watching the game. But not this. In the end they managed an awkward brush of their upper bodies, lasting only seconds before she pulled away. At the bottom of the steps, he turned and raised an arm in farewell. She offered an energetic wave. Gaia. What was she doing? That was way too much. She tried to recover by replicating the English royalty's cupped-hand regal wave, a bit of a joke. But she did it to his back because he was already walking away.

The rest of the week rushed by as she hurried to finish her last few freelance stories, arranged to get out of her office contract and met up with Manu for lunch on Friday. They grabbed sushi takeout and savored it on a bench on the cliffs, looking west across Pacific highway, the beach and out to the ocean.

"You gotta come home for a visit," Manu said. "It's just over there," waving towards TL, "a mere 10,000 kilometres away. We miss you. Vid hook-ups just aren't the same."

"I know. I miss you all too. And you're right vids don't come anywhere near kanohi ki te kanohi." And she meant it. Over nine years, the marae had become her Terra Ludus home, the place she hung out when she needed to get away from basketball and the claustrophobic team atmosphere. Leaving her second family, knowing she might never see many of them again face to face, had been hard.

"Oh yeah, and the Aunties are worried you aren't married yet," Manu added. "Especially Mum. They're threatening to find you a husband if you can't do it yourself."

She laughed freely, imagining Auntie Marama, Auntie Raima and Auntie Jean at one of the long wooden tables in the wharekai, debating the merits of various members of their own and other iwi with whom they shared whakapapa or family connections.

"Oh, I can just see it now. Luckily for me, they'll never agree on anyone, so I'm probably pretty safe."

"Oh yeah? Are you sure? They seem pretty determined. I'd look out if I were you. They're after me to settle down too." Simultaneous looks of horror crossed both their faces but Manu got it into words first, "You don't think...."

"No way! No. Just no. You're like my brother. Yuck!"

"I'd say the same thing," Manu responded, "except I think you'd smack me." They high-fived, in full accord.

A cheeky grin stole across Manu's face. "We could get them going though."

"That'd be fun," she agreed, "but they'd never forgive us. We couldn't do that to them." She shook her head, no. "On a related note, do you want to come over to Simeon's tomorrow to watch the games? You could pretend to be my date! We'll be playing pickup about 14th hour, then have some kai and settle in for the rest of the day. Deltan are playing. It'll be fun."

"Sorry Cuz, can't do it. I'm on the last flight home tonight." As he noted tears suddenly well up in her eyes, he quickly continued. "This was just a short gig. Kind of a trial. I think it went OK so I'm hoping it might turn into something more long-term. You never know." He stood up, ready to go.

She brightened and stood to hug him. "That'd be great. Good luck. You can crash at my place next time if you want. Give the Aunties my love, and tell everyone I miss them. Tell your mom, oops I mean mum, I'm trying to practice the language but it's pretty tough when no-one else speaks it around here."

"E kare, kia kaha. Just do your best," as he held her tight.

"And say hi to Moana." She started to giggle. "At least she's settled down eh? Popping out some mokopuna. Maybe that'll let us off the hook for a bit longer."

"Dream on," was his response to that. Then with a wave and "e noho rā," he was on his way.

EAT SHIT AND DIE

On Saturday, she wore her favorite sweatshirt, worn and washed into faded softness, the DELTS logo barely visible. And her most comfortable workout pants. It was sunny but cold. Perfect for pickup. It might be the last time she'd be allowed out in public dressed this way so she was going to make the most of it. Embrace her current life before it changed. How much she wasn't yet sure but if Imelda's plan worked, and she gave 'good vid', she might not be an anonymous citizen for much longer. Would she have to give up pickup? Surely not. No-one would have to know. And the guys would just get sloppy or not even play at all if she wasn't there to keep them honest.

Her carry bag contained two large bags of salted corn chips, the chilli mince she had cooked last night, a tin of black olives, two ripe avocados, sour cream and a plastic bag of grated cheese, all ready to be heated and combined just before the start. Her icom was in her backpack along with the pad, pens, and highlighters. Simeon had a wireless printer and she'd brought paper from her dwindling stock. Recycled of course but reasonably plentiful thanks to her sources who diverted it to her instead of selling it to the papercyclers.

Simeon met her at the door, steaming black coffee in hand. He must have been waiting for her to arrive. "Come on in. I've got everything set up. Printed out the bulk of them already." He was already in the dining room and she could see printouts stacked in neat piles on the dining table.

"You didn't need to do that."

"Ah but I did. I know how much you like to mess around with paper. And let me guess. You've brought a pad and pens, and colored highlighters in …" he paused, "green, purple and yellow. No orange or blue. Right?"

"Right you are. And wrong. I've got green, purple and yellow, but I didn't want you to miss out on the fun, so I included orange and blue." She laughed. "Not so smart, this morning eh?"

"Hah, hah funny girl. Come on then, let's get started."

"I'll just stick the nacho bits in the fridge." She didn't really want to start. She'd even avoided breakfast just in case. Just hydrated with one cup of jasmine tea. But black coffee should be safe enough.

"Come on. Don't lollygag about. Quicker we start, quicker it's done. And I assume you want it all done and dusted before the guys arrive. So get in here."

It took them two hours just to do the first read through. Simeon suggested five main categories, one for each color. Green for strong support, Yellow or Orange for lukewarm or neutral, and Purple or Blue for negative. They sat side by side, pens between them.

"Rules of engagement," Simeon said. "No grabbing the pens. Be patient if the one you want is being used or just write the first letter beside the comment. Yellow for lukewarm and Orange for neutral. Purple and Blue for negative, with Blue for trolls. One pile at a time, then a break. OK?" She nodded. There were eight stacks, four each. "There's about 125 pages per stack, about five comments per page, depends on how much they wrote," Simeon said. "So it'll take a while. I've got chocolate brownies for the breaks. They say chocolate is a good pick me up."

"I've got a bad feeling we'll need it," she replied, humoring him but unable to imagine eating anything.

"Deep breath. Shoulders back. Gird your loins. Ready, set, go." Simeon grabbed his first sheet, read fast and immediately grabbed the blue highlighter. Her heart sank, the knot in her stomach tightening.

Her first page was alright. Early comments from her vid. Two greens, two yellows and a purple. The second was similar. Two neutrals, and three mildly negatives. It looked like Simeon hadn't put down the blue, except to ask for the purple. He was working on comments from the Ludus Ludus blog, the ones that made her throw up. He was quiet, a vertical frown creased between his eyebrows. After 10 minutes and about five pages, he stood up. "Can you cope with some music? I need something happy."

"No words," she said. "I won't be able to concentrate. You got anything like acoustic guitar?"

"Know just the thing," as he scrolled through his musix options. Then something Spanish-influenced, upbeat and cheerful, brightened the room.

They went back to work. Danny tried not to read any comments in depth. The plan was to pre-organize through color-coding and then go back to extract the content of the commentary. But it was hard not to. She couldn't help glancing at Simeon's coding. Far too much purple and blue for her liking and his frown was still in place. Hers were a wide mix. The initial green domination was slowly disappearing, oranges were still common while purples and blues were starting to build up. What she noticed was the increasing number of exclamation marks and capital letters. That meant shouting, a protocol established right at the start of email, the first instant Int-com, way back. She'd done a story on it last year. Hard to imagine that people had to make decisions about what things meant. It was all so taken-for-granted now.

She heard a snigger from beside her, quickly suppressed. Simeon wasn't supposed to be doing truly focused reading either. Then another snigger escaped.

"What is it? You can't keep it to yourself. Share."

"I don't know if you'll like it though. It's just that some of these trolls are seriously deranged. You just can't take them seriously."

"So you're laughing at blues?"

"Right you are. Blue trolls, little men with no imagination and most likely very little Int-tellect," Simeon laughed at his own joke. "Seriously. They are idiots. There's a lot of them though."

Danny sighed. "Spit it out then. I can handle it." *I hope* she added silently.

"Right. Here's the one that set me off. Don't know if it's really funny but on top of all the rest, it just stood out. So, for the moment, I choose this as my quote of the day. 'Eat shit and die'." He gauged Danny's reaction.

"That's it? The whole comment? That's funny?"

"See. That's what I mean. It's out of context. But it's still funny. What the prig does that mean? Eat shit and die? It's got nothing to do with what you said. There's no thought, no reflection, no connection to the overall discussion. Just like he woke up and decided to take a dump on the conversation." Simeon's snuffling laughter permeated the room again. He always found his own jokes entertaining.

Danny wasn't laughing though. He'd said there were a lot of them. And there were a few in her pile too. Words like bitch and stupid and lez-bro and crap still glittered in her vision although she had tried to move quickly through them into more supportive comments. But the heat of the underlying emotions seared the words into her mind.

"Don't worry. Comments like this have no substance. Think of them like farts. They make a smell, stink up the place then blow away, leaving no trace. It probably wouldn't matter what the topic was, trolls like this are just mad at the world and want an outlet. So they dump all over. They're like untethered flitters on full speed, careering round the Int, dropping packets of vitriol. So they're funny. Stupid-funny. Bozo-funny. Don't-you-have-anything-better-to-do-with-your-life-funny. Don't pay any attention to them. It's not about you. And we're only coding them so you can write a report for NBB. Imagine they're about somebody or something else."

"Easy for you to say," she replied. "I don't know how to make sense of this kind of stuff. It feels pretty personal to me."

"Well it's not. They don't know you from a slab of cheese. And that's about the quality of what's going on in their heads. Even with auto-spell half of them manage to word-mangle. So let's just get on with it. We'll finish the initial sort, then shoot some hoops and watch the game, drink some beer, talk b.s. for a few hours. OK?"

By thirteenth hour they had finished three-quarters of the piles. Danny was focused but down as she pressed on through a lot of nastiness, along with some surprisingly strong responses from supporters. She was coming to realize she might not have to fight this on her own. But as the coding dragged on, even Simeon had stopped laughing. The happy music continued unabated but neither of them paid attention. This was a marathon and the miles were grinding them down. When Danny came across one that ended PRIGGIN DYE BITCH!!!! she realized she'd had enough.

"I've got to stop. I can't take much more of this. Sorry." She left the sheet lying on the table and walked into the kitchen. Turned on the kettle. Turned it off again. She needed to move, to shift her focus, maybe even to swear herself. She paced back and forth, fists clenching and unclenching. She stopped and tried to stretch, to release. Neck stretches and rotations, shoulder rotations, even vigorous hand shaking didn't seem to do much. She went in search of a basketball.

Simeon found her a few minutes later.

"That last page was pretty full on," he said, finding her in the garage rooting through his storage bins.

"Where's the prigging ball?" was her terse response. "I don't want to talk about it."

"Ah, but I think you do," he prodded. "And anyway, you should have kept going. The next one praised you to the skies. Said something like Daniela was my hero growing up and she's absolutely right. And she knows what's she talking about. Those of you who think that it's OK to abuse someone who's telling the truth need to take a good look at yourselves. She's an expert and she's right. If you don't like what she's saying, don't watch the vid. Do something productive instead of spitting all over the Int where the rest of us have to step over it."

By now Simeon had produced the ball and bounce-passed it over to her. "Surely that makes you feel better."

Somehow it did. With the positive words ringing in her ears, and her fingers caressing the familiar leatherness, something let go, just a little. "Let's warm up before the others get here."

"I'll just lock up," he said. "I've hidden the piles in the hutch. I assume you're not broadcasting this gig to the world."

"Thanks. You're right. Only you, Nance, Vic and Mom and Dad know so far. I think I need to keep it that way for now."

By the time the rest of the guys turned up, Danny was sweating and fully warmed up. She and Simeon had taken turns shooting outside shots, free throws, and layups on the court in his gated apartment complex. She'd tossed up a few high passes for Simeon to dunk. It was the only skill she didn't have. Six foot just wasn't tall enough and she didn't have exceptional leaping ability. She was quick and fast.

Elusive they used to call her. And the ball in her hand knew its way to the hoop.

"Want to play together today? Let's kick some serious ass. I think we both need a win, and the DELTS aren't likely to provide it."

She and Simeon rarely teamed up. Together they were the best pair. Con and Dom were good but they both played the same kind of game. But Simeon was right. She needed a win. And it sounded like he did too.

And they won. A lot. Handsomely one might say. Not that they officially kept score. But they all knew. Con and Dom didn't argue about the teams. They read something in Danny's body language that suggested they should just get on with it. And she took it to them. She wanted contact. She wanted bruises. She wanted pain. Theirs or hers. It didn't matter.

They finished just in time for tip-off. Mike was already settled, prime seat as usual. "Where's the nachos?" was his first comment.

"You mean you didn't make them for us?" Dom's sarcasm was laid on like thick mayonnaise.

"Yeah, right. Like you expect me to do anything in the kitchen."

"I'll do it." Danny was already pulling the different components out of the cool-drawer, expertly combining them into their favorite first half dish. "Ten minutes and it'll be ready."

"Too late," Mike yelled. "The game'll be half over. Might have to find a new maid."

"You want any today, you'll put up with this one," she retorted striding into the living room. "Now shut up and watch the game. The DELTS are coming out."

She nabbed a beanbag and settled in. It was a hard-fought game, the lead swapping almost every five minutes. "Turn it up," she demanded as the oven beeped that the nachos were ready. In the few minutes she was out of the room, the lead changed again, putting the DELTS in the lead. The whoops drowned out the commentators. "Shut up," she yelled. "I can't hear."

DELTAN were playing well. Much better than usual. Their new center, Bard Branson, wasn't just huge but he could move and he had a light touch. He was truly what they called a young wonderful.

When he sank a 3-pointer to cement the lead just before half-time, they all cheered. Nobody had touched the nachos. It was too close. She was smiling inside and out.

"Hey, the nachos are cold." Dominic's comment sounded something like a demand.

"Heat them up then," she retorted. "You've got legs. The kitchen's over there." She waved in the general direction and added "And grab me a beer as well." She couldn't be bothered moving.

The studio crew came on. They usually paid only the barest attention to half-time but this time Adie Supruniak was being interviewed. A former point guard who played a couple of seasons with Danny until a hamstring injury cut short her career, Adie was still a good friend. She'd gone into broadcasting soon after her retirement. She was everything Int-TV could ever want. Slightly above average height, long, wavy blonde hair, blue eyes, classic good looks. *The opposite of me.* Mike and Simeon were in full flight debating Branson's contribution to the team's dynamics.

"Methinks, he tis a wondrous addition to thy community," Simeon was clearly riffing off Branson's first name and his favorite playwright, the real Bard, Shakespeare.

"For Gaia's sake Sim. Just talk normally. The guy's a star in the making. No doubt about it." Mike was never short of an opinion. And he rarely took any notice of dissent.

"Thy erudite opining ist in agreement with mine assessment," Sim replied. He could be just as pigheaded and was having too much fun trying to have a functional Bardic conversation.

Danny was watching Adie closely – what she was wearing, how she was moving her hands, what her hair and make-up looked like. They had the volume turned down so she couldn't hear what they were discussing. Suddenly, her own face appeared on screen.

"Whoa," the word exploded out of her. The guys eyeballed her and then followed her gaze to the screen. The image changed to her in uniform, holding the league trophy. Maybe seven years ago?

"Volume up. High," Sim articulated clearly. The male studio anchor's voice immediately boomed out through the surround sound speakers. "This is Bartoli at the height of her career, the year she

won MVP and was awarded the prestigious Most Consistent award."
Simeon, Mike and Dominic all swiveled to stare at her, Dom with the
nacho plate now tipping precariously.

"You won Most Consistent? Are you serious?!" Mike's tone
echoed that of a criminal lawyer rounding on an unreliable witness.

"Shut up right now," Sim demanded. "I want to hear this."

"...think about her call to arms?" They could all figure out
what the question was about.

"I think she's right on the currency," Adie said. "Look at your
network. NBB broadcasts more than 160 men's games a season. And
we're lucky if we get to see five women's games, and they're always on
at fifth hour or some time when any normal person would be sleeping."

"But who needs to watch women's ball live? There's no demand
and whoever the fans are, they can download it to watch later. In fact,
all the Int-chat says no-one cares about women's basketball, period."

"Int-chat?" Adie's sarcasm was far from hidden. "Int-chat is
full of folks who are afraid of change. They don't represent everyone.
I know there's an untapped market out there for women's sport. And
what's the most popular sport in Terra Altrix? Basketball. So Daniela's
right. And the time is right. I think you'd be surprised at how much
interest there would be, once folks have a chance to see the women
play. It's high quality ball and more interesting than the men by far."

The anchor's face registered disbelief the same time as Mike
chortled. "More interesting? Pfiffle."

"Shut up Mike," Simeon demanded as the studio anchor made
a studious attempt at professionalism. "More interesting? Tell us why."

"Well, for one thing, the women play a team game. It's not
a set of individuals playing for themselves. So it's more interesting.
Strategy is more important. Check out a women's game and you get to
see how to use passing to create open space. It's fast, tight and tough."

"But what about dunking? Most women can't get near the
rim."

"So?" Adie wasn't taking the standard approach at all. "What's
so special about dunking? It's all show and no substance. It's not real
basketball."

By now the anchor was struggling to maintain the required neutral stance. The camera kept coming back to his bemused and disbelieving expression. In one shot, his mouth fell open. He couldn't seem to find any way to react. So Adie kept going. Danny knew her well enough to see the subtle signs that she was enjoying herself. And Danny was thinking hard about Adie's arguments. They sounded an awful lot like the ones on her vid, and that she'd talked through with Imelda. Then it hit her. Of course. Adie was seeding the ideas. Putting them out there. Preparing the basketball public for next week's announcement. Pretty damn impressive actually. So she wouldn't be alone. Adie was on her side, and she was well-liked and respected in basketball circles, both male and female. Maybe it would be alright.

"Real basketball," Adie continued, smiling openly now, "is about strategy and exploitation of space on the court. About creating it, and defending it. The open shot is the most beautiful thing because it means the player has bamboozled the defender, left her or him stranded, shown them up. Swish," and she demonstrated perfect technique with her imaginary shot.

"Well," the anchor responded, relief suffusing his features. "We're just about out of time. Thanks to Adie Supruniak for her thought-provoking conversation. After some wonderful promotions from our sponsors, we'll be back to the stadium."

All four guys immediately turned to Danny but Mike spoke first.

"Most Consistent? You never told us that. No-one earns Most Consistent. How come we don't know this?" Mike's voice was rising towards hysteria. He was Mr Stats. Thought he knew everything.

"It's old news," she said. "And why do *you* think you don't know about it? Weren't you listening?"

"But that's bullshit. Most Consistent is the rarest award. You must have been a seriously kick-ass athlete."

"Still am, which you'd know if you ever bothered to come out and play."

"Might have to do that," he muttered before returning to the point. "So what were your stats?"

"Guess." She wanted him to think about it. What it would take to average at least 10 per game over five years in three categories: points, assists and rebounds. What Mike and the others didn't know was that she had averaged above 10 in all three, mostly due to two seasons when Canestri Mulier were so dominant that they regularly won by more than 30 points. But she didn't have to tell them that part. Mike was looking pained. Too much thinking didn't enhance his looks. "Brain hurting?" she joked. "Come on, Stats-man. You've got 30 seconds. You three can guess too. Whoever's furthest away is buying us all dinner. In fact, to avoid cheating, you can each write them down. Keep thinking." She walked into the dining room, pulled a recycled sheet from the hutch and tore it into four pieces. Each of them got a highlighter.

She read Mike's aloud first: "10 points, 10 assists, 10 rebounds." He'd chosen the lowest possible options. She'd known he wouldn't be able to slough off his inherent deficit beliefs about women's sport.

Then Dominic: "20 points, 10 assists, 10 rebounds." He knew she could shoot.

Constantin refused to play. "Oh come on. Don't be a baby," she encouraged him. His hands went nowhere near the paper and pen. "Come on."

"If I have to, I say tens across the board," he said. "No. Scratch that. I'll say you averaged 12 points, 10 for the other two."

Simeon looked confident as she perused his answers: "25 points, 15 assists, 11 rebounds."

She raised her index finger, ran it past their expectant faces, drew a large circle and began to narrow it. Her finger ended pointing at Simeon. "Closest," she said. "And in fact very close. My five-year average was 24 points, 15 assists – good guess – 12 rebounds."

"No way," Mike was incredulous. "Ten plus in all three? That's higher than most of the guys. And those guys are heroes."

"And don't I know it," she retorted.

He was still talking. "You must be the best woman who's ever played."

"Not quite," she said. "But I'm still number 2. If I'd played another year, with the team we had, I might have been number one, but they cut the whole league. So that was that. It was all over for me. Out I went, along with everyone else. Back to Terra Altrix and reality. And, by the way, you're buying dinner."

By now the second half was into its third minute. They turned back to the screen, the real reason they were there. Simeon gave her a wink. She returned it and reclaimed her beanbag.

After dinner, with the compostable sugarcane containers of Thai-Fusion cuisine littering Simeon's coffee table, they discussed the unexpected DELTS win. Group conclusion: the new center was the missing piece of the puzzle and if he stayed healthy and the others stepped up, the DELTS might even reach a winning percentage for the season. Danny kept feeling Mike's eyes on her. Unaccountably quiet, he kept shaking his head, an unconscious 'no' passing across his face. It was disconcerting. Mike never really looked at her. She was part of the furniture, they all were. She imagined herself as a holy relic suddenly dumped into Simeon's modern living room.

"Stop it," she addressed him directly. "Stop staring."

"Staring at what?" He looked genuinely bemused. She realized he wasn't aware of the physical expression of his thoughts.

"You keep staring at me like I'm some exotic animal in the zoo. And you keep shaking your head, like you're thinking No. No. No."

His sudden stillness showed her she was on the right track. Then he relaxed and grinned. "You're right. I am thinking no, no, no. I can't get my head around the fact that I didn't know your stats. That you should be on the list of superstars. And that other woman as well." He paused, a real frown evident now as a new thought occurred to him. "Are there any more? Any more Most Consistents?"

"Not that I know of," she said. "But I think there are three or four others with good numbers, mostly from the early days when the league was a bit more uneven in quality. But the award didn't exist then so I don't know if they count."

"Three or four others?" He clearly couldn't believe the gap in his knowledge base.

"Oooh. Oooh. Mikey doesn't know everything," Constantin jeered. "How can you live with yourself when there's a whole world of stats out there you haven't got stuffed in that big head of yours?"

Danny realized Mike wasn't questioning the validity of the stats themselves, just that they were so invisible. She'd unconsciously expected him to reject her records as invalid because they belonged to women. But he wasn't at all. And if Mike could see things this way, perhaps others would too. As if there was a whole world of arcane information they could add to their knowledge bases. Maybe new questions for sport quiz nights. Who knows? Maybe even joint awards ceremonies for both leagues. She'd have to add this to her arguments for Imelda. Come up with some quiz questions. Perhaps put Mike on it rather than doing the work herself.

"Hey Mike," she said. "If I give you the data, would you come up with some quiz questions on them? Questions about the individuals themselves, and some that compare with all athletes?" You could run them by your quiz night guys – maybe win even more convincingly than usual!"

"Good thinking. We've got one coming up. I'll run them by you and put them in." He lay back, eyes closed. "I can see it now. 'How many basketball athletes have reached the Most Consistent in all three categories?' The usual answer is five. But the real answer now is seven. And our team will be the only one to get it. Then they'll all be yelling that it's not true. And I'll be able to prove why they're wrong."

She knew he loved being right, loved having found some piece of history or information that no-one else had. Unexpectedly, she'd given him extra ammunition to enhance his own status and he was embracing it. It probably didn't mean he cared about the women's game but did that matter? If he could see it as a resource for his own life, he might still support the league having a higher profile.

"You up for it boys?" he asked, looking at the other three. "We'll smash it this week."

Simeon looked up. "What night?" His sideways glance at Danny let her know he was thinking ahead.

"Thursday at Jambos. You coming?"

"Not sure," Simeon replied, now looking pointedly at Danny. Turning back to Mike, "Do you need me?"

"Probably not. Can you come Danny? It'd look better if it seemed like you were giving the answers."

"Sorry. Got something on. You go for it though. I'd love to see their faces when you show them up." She reinforced the reason she thought he was on board and he lit up.

"Yeah. The Smart-Asses'll crap their little pants." Mike had an intense competition going with one other team, filled with rabid basketball fans like himself. They competed to add new quiz questions, and Danny had been to enough quiz nights that she knew they fought like pigs and dogs over every new answer. Evidence would be needed.

"I'll give you the contact details for the current Canestri Mulier coach, Denise Herington," she told him. "I used to play with her and she's also the archivist for the women's game. She'll be happy to help you out."

"Excellent. I'll get on it. New questions have to be in by Tuesday."

She stayed to help Simeon clean up. "That went well," he said. "Never thought Mike would react like that. And how come you never told us? Those are really important records."

"Couldn't face the thought of Mike's ridicule. And I don't know. I like the way things are. I didn't want to spoil it." The words were out before she could stop them. But they were true. She really didn't want to throw a spanner in the works, upset the apple cart, queer the pitch – all the family phrases came to mind. *What the hell did they all mean anyway? Queer the pitch? Upset the apple cart?* She couldn't ever remember seeing an apple cart. *Oh well, random thought string. Doesn't matter.*

He considered it. "Will it change things? Wasted worry I think," he said, wiping a still slightly greasy container. "Except Mike might start wanting to play!" He biffed the container in the general direction of the composting bin. "It doesn't worry me. In fact it makes me feel better about being outplayed so often. Now I can say that I play pickup with a legend. That I lose to a legend. That's kind of cool."

She handed him a lid after shaking off the biodegradable sea-friendly soapsuds. "Really?"

"Yeah. Really. Not many people ever get to play with a legend. Who's the other one? Is she still alive?"

"No. She passed over the year after I broke her record. Some kind of zoomer accident. Nothing left but DNA to identify her. It was quite a big story at the time. But maybe not, or Mike would have known about her. Maybe it was just in our circles."

"Hey. You could play some charity matches. 'Roll up. Roll Up. Go one-on-one with a basketball legend. Bring your friends. Bring your family.' Hah!" She dropped what she was washing at his sudden shout. Luckily it wasn't breakable, only a container lid.

"I've got it. You go one-on-one with each of us – or maybe we play 2-on-2. Mike can make a vid and we'll post it. Seed it. It'll go viral. What do you think?"

She liked the idea but she'd have to run it by Imelda. "Let me check it out with the powers that be. I'm going back down on Tuesday. They might like it actually."

"Tuesday hey? That means you've got to get your analysis done by then. What are your plans for tomorrow? I'm free." He stopped. Then continued. "If you need me of course."

"Of course I need you. I can't do this by myself. I appreciate your analytic skills." *Gaia I sound like a wanker*. Switching to a slow, fake cowboy voice, she went on. "You think good. Me like."

"OK then. Tenth hour again?" It was already twentieth hour and she needed to get home and sleep. They finished the dishes. She wiped the bench to catch the last drops of water.

"Sure. Want me to bring croissants? Chocolate?"

"How can I refuse an offer like that? Sure. I'll make the coffee. Got a new blend with a great kick. It'll keep us going."

THREAT

It was near the end of the last pile. They were both tired. Her eyes were dry and itchy, and a headache was immanent. It looked like another positive so she took time to read it. 'You're a clever girl and I'm sure you love b-ball,' it began. Her hackles raised a bit at the 'girl' – probably an older man still resisting gender equality – but she did love her sport. The comment continued. 'Let me explain this to you clearly. Basketball is a man's game. *The* man's game.' *Here we go. The same old chestnut. Sounds like an old-school sexist,* and she reached for the purple highlighter. "Women can play but only an inferior version, a spectacle something akin to a robot having sex. Interesting enough as a concept but so far from the real thing that it's incomprehensible that a major broadcaster would sully the sport by showing it. Rather than b-ball it would be nothing other than fee-ball. If NBB buy your 'public responsibility' argument and try to introduce it, I will hold you responsible."

It was her stillness that gave her away, the words holding her in their grip. Simeon turned, his hands reaching towards hers. She didn't realize they were clenched shut until he wrapped both of his – so warm – around them.

"What's wrong? You're as white as that piece of parchment." He squeezed both fists, massaging, loosening her fingers.

She wasn't sure it was possible to breathe. She didn't answer, just kept staring at the words unfolding, letter by letter, word by word. 'I know where you live. And where you work. Nice cat by the way. A bit timid but nothing a fresh piece of meat won't fix. Stop this feminist nonsense or else.'

Simeon was reading too.

"What do I do?" she whispered. "Oh Bumbles." Tears threatened. "Prig."

"Prigging bastard you mean." Simeon's voice was hard. His attempted reassuring smile did little. She could see the tightness around his lips, the way his smile looked pasted on. She took another deep breath. *Must keep doing that.*

"It's real, isn't it? That threat. He's not just a bloggart." Even the pseudo, Real Man, sounded dangerous.

"Right," Simeon said. "Look at me." He waited until she made eye contact. "It's probably not real, just written in a way to make you think that."

"But he knows I have a cat."

"So do lots of other people. You post pix and vids of him on your vlog for Gaia's sake. It's not an Admin secret." Simeon removed his arm that had somehow crept around her shoulders. She shivered at the sudden loss of warmth. She didn't seem to be able to generate any heat of her own.

"Stay there," he said, removing the parchment and taking it into the kitchen. He quickly returned with a reheated eggnog-chai she'd brought with her this morning, with the addition of two pink marshmallows floating on top.

"Ugh. I hate pink ones."

"Take them out then."

"No white ones?"

"Nope. Only pink. Sorry."

The offending pinks removed, she took a sip. Just the right temperature, warming the mouth but not burning the tongue, gentle heat down her throat and settling in her center, slowly returning her to normal. Unaccountably, she believed Simeon. But she'd remove all evidence of Bumbles and make sure her address wasn't online anywhere public. She couldn't do much about work but she wasn't likely to be there much.

"It's not real," he said. "Psychia didn't pick it up, did it?" No it hadn't. She'd run all the comments through the program and nothing unusual came up.

"But you better use it as one of your examples. So that NBB knows how some people feel."

He was right. It was only one of hundreds that said the same thing. The 'I know where you live' had thrown her but surely that was just because that's what all the creepy vid stalkers always said.

"I'll finish them off," he said. "You just sit there and relax. We're nearly done. Or you can take the piles we've done and read through all the greens. Feel better. Forget that dropkick."

It seemed like a good idea. But reading the positives didn't have any effect. The clenched ball in her stomach still felt like threat. Felt real. And then she realized why. She hadn't set Psychia's parameters to pick up threats. She'd asked for top-level categorization into one of the five categories only.

"I didn't ask Psychia for threats," she said. "I just went for the basic sort."

"Do you want to run it again? I've got enough bandwidth left for this week, 20 minutes maybe. It might be enough."

They agreed to run only the major alert (red level) over the whole data set. Psychia had already been over it once, and this time it would only be looking for major threats to the wellbeing of her or others, including self-harm. She sent a little message to Gaia that nothing would trigger, especially not this message.

The ping of completion turned her blood cold. She knew what it was. She'd heard that sound once before when she attracted a stalker, after she wrote a story on modern-day sex, who seemed to think that she had hidden desires only he could fulfill. He turned out to be harmless, slightly mind-unbalanced, so hormonal therapy rather than isolation was the solution.

This felt qualitatively different. Not the slightly offbeat goofiness of before, but something icier and meaner.

Simeon perused the result in silence. "Better contact the peacekeepers," he suggested. But she didn't want to, not before NBB made the announcement.

"Can we just keep it quiet 'til next week? I'll tell NBB on Tuesday when I zoom for my meeting."

"And in the meantime?"

"Well. There's nothing to trigger the threat. At least not yet." She didn't want to leave Simeon's house. But there was Bumbles, and he needed protection much more than she did. It was already dark and the thought of driving home to an empty apartment was not appealing. Her thoughts must have shown on her face.

"Do you want me to follow you home? No, scratch that," he said. She froze as a spike of fear lurched through her, like an unexpected electric shock. He wasn't going to help. Could she ask him outright?

"I don't like this," he continued. "If you're not going to follow up with the peacekeepers, then you're going to have to put up with me." Her quizzical look kept him talking. "I'm coming over. I can sleep on the couch. It was comfy enough. You and Bumbles need company." She liked that he didn't say protection.

"I've been taking care of myself, and Bumbles, for a long time," she felt necessary to point out.

"I know. It's not a criticism. But I'm worried and I won't be able to sleep if you're on your own. Humor me, OK?

He'd given her an elegant retrieval of face. "Well, if you put it that way, then you're welcome. Bumbles was rather taken with you so I doubt if he'll mind much." She wouldn't mind either. In fact, it was more than that. She wanted him there.

"Let's pack up all this parchment and head over. I'll follow you. Lock the doors and don't get out of your car until I'm there."

Gaia. He was taking it seriously. She didn't know if this made her feel better or worse.

In her living room with the lights on daytime setting and the blinds down, all this worry felt silly. "You don't need to stay," she ventured.

"I know." He dropped his overnight bag behind the couch. "But I am anyway. Now, I wonder if there's a replay. Int on." As the 50-inch screen blazed into life, he talked it through the sports channels. "75. Crap. Who the hell wants to watch golf? 77. Yesterday's game. Know that result. 79. Ah. That'll do." And he relaxed and ordered an Int window. "Daniela Bartoli." And there he sat, checking out the latest posts. She couldn't watch so she headed to the kitchen to top up Bumble's food and water. He was always keen for something just a little bit fresher.

"Still trending," Simeon spoke loudly. "You're up to 3 million hits. That's another 500,000 on top of the initial Psychia sort."

She could tell he was scanning them. A couple of snorts, a harrumph, and some longer silences. "Nothing new," he updated her. "Pretty much what we've already seen. Getting quite bi-polar though. And they're arguing with each other. Your vid's really got something going. Don't know if some of these people are really fans of women's ball or just prigged off at the bozos but they're talking pretty positively. Then they get shouted at. But some of them are shouting back. And there seems to be some kind of fight over b-ball versus fee-ball. Your guy meant it as an insult..."

"He's not my guy."

"Sorry. That guy meant it as an insult but someone reframed it as a short for femme-ball and has reclaimed it. Listen to this. 'Fe-ball is the opposite of feeble. Strategic. Clever. Feminine. What more could you morons want? Fe-ball is everything b-ball should be.' Hah! That shut them up. That thread died. Now. Onto something more important. How long will you be in Mountain View?"

"I'm supposed to be heading up on Tuesday for the week. Planning to zoom-write the summary draft on the way. But I don't know if I should go."

"Of course you should go. I'll stay here," he said. "I've got a few days leave. Dubai Open is coming up. Bumbles and I can bet on tennis and get drunk on beer and cat-milk. I'll be drinking the beer," he clarified.

"I can't ask you to take leave," she responded. "And what if this is a real threat? He could come after you." The thought horrified her. It clearly had not occurred to him either.

"Right. Change of plan. How about I take Bumbles to my place and you come there when you get back? When will you be back, by the way?"

"I don't actually know. I'm likely to be there all week. My contract says I have to be available 24 hours a day, whatever that means. And if they keep me all week, that's much too long for you to take care of him."

"What's he like in a new place?" Simeon ignored her last comment.

"Alright I think. He's stayed at Mom and Dad's a couple of times. But they're in the rurality. You could just keep him inside. I've got a litter box and stuff. Just keep it in the garage or an enclosed space."

She smiled at Simeon's nose twitch and moue of disgust.

"It's easy. Just clean it out once a day. Bin and replace." She talked him through it. And it was agreed. Tonight at her place. Tomorrow they would move Bumbles together and she'd stay over – her turn on the couch – to settle Bumbles in.

She slept badly, cuddled up to Bumbles who didn't resist, given that nighttime temperatures were still cool. The next morning, they decamped, making the several trips back and forth to the cars together, neither wanting to leave the other alone.

"I really appreciate this," she said, locking the front door. "Nancy or Vic could come and feed him, or even my next-door neighbor, but no-one can stay at the apartment. And I can't bear the thought of someone breaking in and hurting him."

"Don't worry," he said. "Now, on the way to my place, let's pretend we're spies. We'll take some sneaky back streets, check no-one is following us, double-back. It'll be fun. Then I'll get you both settled in and head to work."

"Both of us?"

"Yes. You don't want to go to work do you?"

Not really. But she needed bandwidth today. She'd need Psychia's summarizing and sorting power.

"You can use my bandwidth," he said, knowing what she was thinking. "I get a special deal. Just don't stay on Psychia all day." He did some kind of Int security for a lot of big corps. He never discussed his job, always displaced direct questions with a joke of some sort. But one of them must be the connection that got him extra supply. She'd take it.

GETTING READY

On Tuesday, she was given 30 minutes with Imelda after arriving at tenth hour. She'd shared the summary. First the blues and purples, 72% against, another 8% neutral, with the most common argument being some variation of basketball is a man's game, women can't play or women aren't as good as men so why bother. The surprisingly strong 20% in favor of the idea (the greens) showed there was definitely a market, albeit a small one. Imelda didn't seem concerned about the 'I know where you live' post, saying they'd seen plenty of them in the past and nothing ever came of it.

"Gives them a place to vent their spleen," she said. "That seems to be enough."

Things had moved fast. The launch was set for the Friday evening news hour. She'd be interviewed this afternoon for a worldwide release. That's why the makeup and studio lessons were needed. They wanted her to do a session in the gym with her old team on Wednesday. So she'd flit to Terra Ludus tomorrow.

"Hope you've been practicing." Imelda was only half-joking.

"Play every weekend," she replied. "So most of the basics are still there. I don't know if I'm fit enough to go up against the pros though."

"Don't worry about that. We'll edit it to make you look good."

Danny hoped the players were on board with that idea. She'd have to talk to Denise, the Canestri Mulier coach, and make sure. It should help that they knew each other well.

At eleventh hour she found herself in an upright leather chair, almost blinded by the bright lights surrounding the large mirror she was facing. Emilie de Tourney was talking her through the basic daily makeup routine she'd be required to follow on her days off. Danny figured Emilie had decided to start gently, with something closer to Danny's usual 'natural' look. After only half an hour, she'd realized that natural was something close to a curseword, the slight curling of Emilie's upper lip every time she said it a dead giveaway.

"Do I really have to wear foundation every day?" She couldn't help the slightly plaintive intonation. "My skin's naturally pretty blemish-free." She also couldn't help herself throwing 'natural' into the conversation just to see the reaction.

Emilie cocked her head, moved closer, so close in fact that Danny could feel her warm breath on her face. After an extended observation, she straightened.

"OK. Here's the compromise. You'll wear a daily moisturizer with a cream foundation included. You'll barely know it's there but it will give you a smooth cover in case you're snapped by the public or papps."

"Paparazzi? Me?" She couldn't believe that would be the case.

"You'll be surprised," Emilie replied. "As soon as you're on Int screens, they start swarming. Especially for someone as 'naturally' (heavy on the sarcasm there) beautiful as you."

Danny didn't know what to respond to first. The 'on screens' or the 'beautiful'. Both seemed ludicrous. The confusion must have been evident because Emilie continued. "Look. Everyone on Int-TV becomes famous at some level. And the public want to know about their lives so you need to be prepared for that. If you turn out to be a minor or a micro – famous in just one area – then the interest will probably be limited just to you, not your family or friends. In your case, I think it will be more than that. Photogenics have a lot of do with it."

"Photogenic? Me?" Danny was shaking her head.

"No doubt. Look, here's how it works. Most photogenics look pretty normal in everyday life. But something about the balance of their features sings to the lens. They come alive, communicate. And you're one of those. I've seen your vid. You've really got it. And my job is to enhance it. To make sure you look good all the time. Which means three different looks. One for everyday – that's what we're working on now. One for evening. One for on screen. All need different combinations."

"But …" Danny needed to say something, she just wasn't sure what it was.

"But nothing. It's pretty clear you don't usually wear much makeup. So don't worry, I'm not going to turn you into a painted doll. And you did an OK job on your vid choices. Like I said, I'm here to enhance what you've got, not make you into some kind of a caricature." Her voice quietened to a whisper. "You've got a really unique look, not like all those blonde dollies who read the news. Let's blow them out of the water."

Danny was beginning to realize that she was working with someone as passionate about makeup as she was about basketball. *What the hell. Let her do her stuff. And maybe it won't be too bad. Better to work with her than fight it.*

"Alright. Let's do it. Make me gorgeous!"

Three hours later, she left with three makeup bags. Yellow for day. Dark blue for night. Pink for on-screen (Emilie's nod to femme). A set of vids and pix of how to apply each one (shot once Emilie was satisfied with each look). Emilie made her practice, applying each look twice. Three times for on-screen because she couldn't quite get the foundation thickness right. It felt too much like applying a mud-mask, even though it moved fluidly and didn't affect her expressions, so she unconsciously resisted putting that much gunk on her skin.

"Don't worry about this one too much," Emilie said. "There'll always be someone like me to put it on for you. But bring the bag and the finished pix every time. And I mean every time. Some of these bozettes (the female of bozo Danny assumed) will try to fit your look into the current 'box' and it won't work. You're different and I want to celebrate that. Don't let them mess with the look." Danny nodded.

"You go girl. Knock 'em dead," were Emilie's parting words, as Danny headed towards the studio for training, fully made up.

The studio practice lasted two hours. They taught her how to sit, hold her hands, how and when to smile, when to turn towards the interviewer, and when to speak directly to the camera. Then she did her first go-live with one of the blonde dollies (Emilie had explained that dollies wasn't gendered). The immaculately coiffed male sports editor asked her some questions and she answered as best she could.

There was so much to concentrate on. Then she discussed the questions and her answers with NBB's news director, Abe Newmann. The first go-live was good, he told her but there were things she could work on. So she practiced. And they did another take. And practiced. And did another take. And another. It was exhausting. Finally, Abe was satisfied that he had enough vid to work with.

"Not as easy as you thought, eh?" Abe gave her a wry smile. "Watching on the Int, it looks easy but it's not. It's a steep learning curve and you've done well today. Someone will be with you tomorrow as well."

"You mean we'll have to go over and over things again?" she couldn't quite keep the horror out of her voice. It was like being an actor. She thought news was news. Live, as it happened. Apparently not.

"Yes you will. Even the basketball shots might need quite a few takes. It's just how Int-TV works. Our job is to make it look plausibly live. But whenever possible, we'll control what happens, the framing of the images, what the talent says. That's you by the way, the talent," he added.

She drew in and blew out a deep breath. *What have I got myself into?*

"Don't worry. You're actually a natural," he said, meaning it as a compliment. "Your pacing is on target, and you project your voice well. It doesn't sound forced."

"It didn't feel like it in there. We had to do everything five times."

"That's not very many," he explained. "Sometimes it takes 20 or more. But most of yours were useable. Our techies just like having some options. Get a good night's sleep and someone will pick you up at sixth hour." He walked away, leaving her at the front desk where an Escort waited to take her back to the same hotel as last time.

BACK ON THE COURT

The light-alarm eased her out of a deep well of mental exhaustion. She hadn't even had time to vid anyone before she passed out, after responsibly removing her studio make-up. Emilie had been insistent. Take it off ASAP, every time, or she'd wreck her skin.

She'd had it easy the last few years. Getting up when she wanted, pursuing stories she was interested in, making her own hours. She had the journalism skills down pat. This Int-TV business was a whole new game.

It was too early to live-vid so she made a short audio packet saying all was well, her brain was hurting, and she was heading to Terra Ludus and didn't know when she'd be back. She said to make sure to watch Friday night's NBB news hour. That was as far as she could go. And she shared it with her parents, Nancy, Vic and Simeon, the only ones who knew what she was doing.

Advances in aviation meant the trip took only three hours. She couldn't imagine what it must have been like in Dad's day, when flights were more than twelve hours from Terra Altrix, and up to 24 or more from the northern regions. High-end Terra Ludus tourism had expanded as travel time decreased even though it was more expensive. It was her first time in a flitter, one of the small, super-expensive, windowless Mach 6 speeders that only major corporations like NBB could afford. The passengers included her, the production manager, a camera guy, and another blonde dolly reporter, a woman this time, who would be asking the questions. *Why are there so many in TV? Do they come off a production line hidden somewhere? Is there a secret breeding program?*

Danny asked her a few basketball questions, wanting to be sure NBB was taking it seriously. To her surprise, the reporter, Sally-Anne Lubic, knew a lot, even though Danny had never seen her on Int-basketball coverage. So Danny threw some of Mike's trickier quiz questions at her. She got most of them right. Then Sally-Anne started questioning her right back. Why had she made the vid? What was she trying to achieve? Why should people care about women's basketball? What made it interesting? How would she answer the naysayers? *No rest in this gig. This is clearly a working flight.* So Danny focused and tried to think what would make 'good vid' as Sally-Anne and the production manager, Arjun Adani, grilled her and helped her refine her answers. She had some advice for them too, on a couple of questions that would be ridiculed in basketball circles. When they suggested that non-basketball fans might find them interesting, Danny protested. "You've got to get the basketball fans on board first," she said. "Without them, you don't have a chance of building an audience." Arjun wasn't convinced. "We're trying to open up new markets with this," he said. "Women, kids, mature-agers. We assume the basketball fans will migrate as a matter of course."

She harrumphed. *Sounding like Mike.* "Not guaranteed," she said. "I've just read more than 5,000 comments on my vid and other blogs. I haven't even looked at the vlogs. And almost three-quarters were against televising the new league. They really feel it's a man's game and women can't play. So we do need to try to get them on board, and I think we can do it two ways." Both leaned towards Danny, interested. *At least they're open.*

"Did you hear Adie Supruniak the other night?" They nodded. "Have you seen my vid?" More nods. "OK then. First, I think we need to make the case that the women's game is a different game – not lesser but different. That's the least controversial. Then, I think we argue that it's the real game. Basketball as it should be played, as it was intended. As strategic, as clever, as a passing game, a smart game, a team game. We don't need to put down the men directly. But emphasizing these aspects will throw the spotlight on the individualistic, show-off, selfishness of the men's elite game. I don't think we need to say that. It will be obvious."

They both nodded, encouraging her to continue. *Wow. They're actually listening. This is great.* Arjun directed his high-kilowatt smile, framed by dark straight hair, smooth tanned skin, sparkling brown eyes and classic features, towards her. He had the looks to be a blonde dolly himself. She wondered why he was behind the camera instead of in front of it.

"And another thing. We need stats. We need to highlight the best women athletes. And the history of the game. How long it's been going. The real stars, both individuals and teams. Especially when their records are better than the men's."

Sally-Anne was smiling, Arjun not quite sure. "Better than the men's?" he ventured.

"Yes. One of my friends is a crazy stats freak. And he nearly had a fit when he found out that two women have Most Consistent records in all three categories. He couldn't believe he didn't know this, and he's off to win another quiz night with his new information. So I think this is another way in."

"Not to mention that you're one of those two," Sally-Anne added. *Kudos to you for doing your homework.* "Daniela is one of the two women, the only one alive, with a Most Consistent award in all 3 categories," Sally-Anne informed Arjun. "We should highlight that today somehow. That's got to go in the news vid. Have we got any old vid of her playing?" Arjun tapped his icom. "We do. There's not much but I'll see if we've got any of the presentation. When was it?"

"Seven years ago," Sally-Anne responded. *More kudos.* "Do you remember if they had cameras?" This was directed at Danny.

"Ah, maybe. I wasn't paying much attention. But I do remember some pix afterwards."

"If we can get it, let's use it." Sally-Anne was clearly taking charge.

"Have you thought about getting some comment from Adie?" Danny addressed this to Arjun. "She's really popular and well-respected in both men's and women's basketball circles." *And another blondie.*

He nodded. "Yes, we've already arranged to film her. She and Ms Consonati are good friends."

Ms Consonati. Maybe I've been a bit forward calling her Imelda. No. She told me to do that. Must check if I can do that in public.

"What do you think?" she asked the camera guy. He hadn't said a word. "What's your background?"

"Korfball," he muttered. "Don't know how I got this gig. Need to be ready for the world champs next week."

Korfball, developed by the Dutch as a gender- and height-neutral game, had many similarities to basketball she realized. Her questioning look was answered by Arjun.

"We didn't want a basketball cam-op," he said. "They'd be too immured in the men's game. Korfball is the closest to how we plan to promote the women's league. The passing, the spatial aspects, the clever dodging, the getting free. The only other option we considered was handball but it doesn't have the vertical aspect. And the world champs are already underway so there was no-one available. Clive here," he said, gesturing towards the cameraman, "is our most experienced korfball vid man."

Clive didn't look impressed at his new assignment.

"Well, I'm glad you're here." She beamed her most welcoming smile in his direction. If Emilie was correct, maybe she could use her 'natural beauty' and flattery to encourage him. "We really need top-class vid. If NBB says you're their best, then I'm happy to be working with you." His smile wasn't exactly spontaneous or complete, but it was a start.

By the time they arrived at the redeveloped basketball complex, she was eager to get started. This could be fun. The warmth of a late summer breeze caressed her bare arms. Looking up, she realized how much she missed the Aotearoa sky, its deep blue punctuated with puffy white clouds. The air was richly scented with flowers. The bell-like calls of a tui rang out, teasing her memories. Sky, life, earth and, surprisingly, a feeling of homecoming. The acid residue of being unwanted had disappeared. She was back and it was for something bigger than herself.

NBB provided her with playing kit, branded with the new league. Very vogue. Pink logo and graphics. *And why not? Embrace the femme rather than fight it.* A stylized female athlete at the top of her jump shot ran up the side of her black leggings. A good choice. The most slimming color and doesn't show the sweat so much. World

Women's League: The Real Deal across her chest. The top was short-sleeved, the latest breathable, body-monitoring and responsive material. Flexible and non-restrictive. NBB had clearly already invested heavily in this concept. This thought took some of the pressure off. *I'm just a cog in the big wheel. Someone who happened to appear at the right time. And so what? If I can help, why not? I don't deserve it but if they need a figurehead, I'll do my best.*

Dressed, she headed into an empty gym in the multi-court complex built after her career ended. *Wow.* Twice the size of when she played, comfortable padded seats, and an impressive ring of corporate boxes. And warm. Just the right temperature. Nothing like the old days when Canestri Mulier practiced in an unheated gym. It was tolerable in summer with the doors open, but in winter they wheeled in massive heating fans that sounded like jet engines taking off but did nothing except slightly moderate the worst of the chill. You definitely wouldn't need hot pads to keep your hands warm while sitting on the bench, let alone blankets. And the floor. *Oh Gaia. It's beautiful.* She jumped a couple of times. Yes. It was sprung with just the right amount of give. She bent down to run her hands over it. Smooth but not slippery. And such an enticing golden glaze over the wood. What would it be like to really play here?

"Hey Danny. Down on the floor as usual eh?" The voice was familiar, as was the reference to Danny's predilection ending up on the ground. She almost always finished games with bruised knees from scrambling after loose balls.

"Kia ora. Hi Denise." They embraced. Out of the corner of her eye, Danny saw the camera's red light. Clive was doing his job. She tried to ignore it, realizing that natural would make the best vid.

"Ready for action?" Denise asked. "They've told us what they want. To make you look good and showcase the best of what we've got."

"Are you alright with that?" Danny needed to be sure. "I don't want to upset the team. Because it's not really about me."

"For sure it's about you," Denise retorted. "But the girls are OK with it. Anything to promote our game. And anyway, half of them are in total awe of you. You're their shero. Our only living legend."

The sarcasm was friendly. Denise had pretty valuable stats in her career too. Even as co-captains, they'd always competed with each other. But because they played different positions, it was more in fun than anything else.

"Well they won't be in awe after today." Danny just hoped she wouldn't be shown up too badly.

"Don't sweat it. We'll make you look good."

"Let's get it on then." They confirmed the decision with a low-five-high-five hand-slap combo (old habits die hard apparently) as the team walked out from the locker room. Denise signaled them over and made the introductions. *Some of these girls are huge. Well over six feet. Guess I ought to be glad I played when I did. I'd be lucky to get a spot as point guard on this team.*

She shook their hands and joked that they should go gently on her because she only played pick-up these days. At least half of them towered over her. Oh well, nothing but her pride to lose. Hopefully Clive would take pity on her. These days anything, and usually everything, made it onto the Int. Privacy was a scarce resource.

They started the warm up and she was expected to slot into the line-up. At least it was familiar. Denise had clearly stuck with their old routines so it didn't take her long to find the rhythm. The sense of home was growing, as she became immersed in the sounds and smells. The squeak of shoes on the freshly varnished floorboards, the resonance of the bounced ball, the scent of well-used leather. At the back of a line waiting for the lay-up drill, with no-one looking, she brought the ball to her nose and inhaled deeply. There was something about basketballs that were used every day – some indefinable odor, a mix of sweat and oil and passion, that instantly transported her back to her professional days. The balls they played with at home didn't smell the same. They were used too infrequently. Once a week for a couple of hours just wasn't enough.

They played a full half while Clive shot vid from a range of angles, including both sidelines, the ends, and high up in the stands, even in a corp-box. Danny rotated into what the girls were calling TD (Team Danny). They were wearing the same black and pink outfits.

The other 'side' were dressed in a deep blue with yellow, the logo reading Canestri Mulier. It felt good to run, to be pushed hard, to bump and be bumped. Good thing she still had a decent long-distance jump shot because she wasn't going to have any success under the basket. The opposition forwards could probably block her shot without even leaving the floor. She landed a few good shots, took a couple of charges and landed on her butt. Got the foul though. But it hurt, no doubt. These girls weren't just fast, they were solid. And she wasn't used to setting real picks and blocks. After what turned out to be a hard-fought half, Team Danny exchanged slick hugs. They were behind but only by 5 points.

Arjun and Clive joined the half-time shared huddle. "Right, we've got a good idea of what's happening, and some good action vid," Arjun stated. "In the second half, we'd like to start to emphasize the style we'll be promoting for the league. The emphasis is on passing, getting open shots, artful dodging." Everyone nodded. Clearly they'd been briefed beforehand. "So you won't be playing a real game exactly. We'll start and stop the clock with each interruption so it will seem real but we might need to set up some moves, especially with Daniela. OK?"

"Fine," said Denise. "Right girls. I want you all to listen up. At least five passes before any shot, unless it's a runaway layup. And I don't want to see any of those because it means you all are not playing defense. Set clean picks, and don't take the shot unless you're open." Speaking directly to her point guard, "Amiria. I want you to look for the lob to Junie for a dunk if it's open, but don't force it." As she saw Arjun frowning, she went on, "I know that's not the focus, but there's nothing wrong with showing that women can dunk too. Amiria, show him" – pointing at Clive – "the signal so he can be ready. Danny. We'll run the old 5–3 move. Do you remember?"

"Can you just go over it with me?"

They walked her through it before the restart. This had clearly been thought out. The opposition (Team CM) were in on the move so they'd play for real but make sure Danny got her open shot. *No pressure.*

They ran the 5–3 twice, left and right. Danny missed one, got the other, a lovely 3-pointer. Then she was benched while the team showed why it was last year's world championship semi-finalists.

While the players retired to the locker room to shower and change, Danny was given a private spot in the referee's office. Her next outfit was laid out. An official league dress shirt in the same colors as her playing uniform. Dress black pants, that flattered her waist but weren't too tight. They fit like a second skin. And her yellow make-up kit and pix. Half an hour later, she was ready.

Sally-Anne was waiting on court, Clive beside her. The interview began, the same questions as they'd practiced on the flight. Sally-Anne added some questions about Danny's assessment of the quality of the players and her experience being back on the court. They did several takes of most of them. Then Denise was invited over and Sally-Anne put some questions to her.

"So, how did Daniela go today," was the first one.

"Not bad for an old girl," Denise said, her broader than usual smile reinforcing the joke. "She fit in real well and she hasn't lost too many of her legendary skills. That was one sweet 3-pointer."

A five second pause was followed by "Well done. That's exactly what we want. The humor works." Sally-Anne checked with Clive that he got the shot. At his nod, she went on.

"So what do you think of the new league?"

"It's fantastic. Women's basketball is undergoing rapid changes and the quality and skill of the athletes is constantly improving. I think people will be surprised at just how spectacular the women's game is. We can't wait."

Another pause. "Another good answer. I think that's enough for now. Thanks Denise. We really appreciate it."

"Don't thank me," Denise replied. "We're happy to do whatever you all need. This is the best thing that could happen for our game and we're with you all the way."

"OK. Thanks. Well. Time to go. Gotta get Danny back for the promotional activities." Looking towards Clive. "You done? All uploaded?" At his nod – clearly a cam-op who didn't talk much – she turned back to Denise. "Launch is Friday night NBB news hour.

Keep that under your hat though. Just be ready for media calls. We've left the media guides and briefing documents with your administrator. Make sure the girls are prepped."

Danny and Denise hugged farewell. "Thanks," Denise whispered. "And don't worry about the bozos. We know they're out there. Just go out and show them what you're made of. Remember you'll always be a legend. The best there is."

TRAINING

After a late-evening return to Mountain View, Thursday and Friday involved training, training, training. Not the physical kind, which she liked, but studio work. First up was being the interviewer, learning how to divide her mind so she could listen to the director in the earpiece while asking questions. Then there was learning to read the autocue, how to engage with material on the vid wall behind her and when to turn back to her camera. It took some doing. At first she would stop, a look on her face like a deer in the zoom-lights, then try to recover and continue. They replayed these beginnings to the whole studio crew at lunchtime – a bit of light entertainment at her expense. But just when she was beginning to feel hopeless, they added a few early clips from Sally-Anne and Adie and even the male sports editor who would interview her on Friday. They looked just like Danny but now they were so professional. More laughter and Sally-Anne joined in. So, it was just a new skill, like learning how to do a layup. To finish, they played her last clip, when the director and sports reporter had collaborated to try and trip her up. She didn't fall for it. She'd got her system going – pay full attention to who she was interviewing, and think of the director like the voice of her conscience, to be heard and acted on when appropriate but definitely in position number 2. She didn't share this conception with them, wasn't sure it was the right hierarchy, but it kept her focused. The crew clapped and mock-bowed to her as she kept her cool on screen.

The afternoon and next morning involved more practice, this time as the interviewee, planning answers to both expected and unexpected questions. She handled the basketball ones but had to stop herself from doing the goldfish impression when Arjun asked, "So have you ever been in a lesbian relationship?" She activated the standard answer to give her time to think. "That's an interesting question Arjun" (they had taught her to use the reporter's name whenever possible in such situations because it reduced the likelihood it would be picked up by other media). Her brain working overtime, she continued, "Could you explain why you think it's an important question to ask at this time?" (They also taught her to turn inappropriate questions politely back onto the reporter).

Arjun gave her a spontaneous thumbs-up as he continued his questions. "Well, Ms Bartoli, it's that we think our viewers would like to know more about you."

"What I can tell you," she replied, "is that I am not in a relationship at the moment." She refused to fall into the trap of defending herself, of claiming the privilege of her heterosexual orientation. Enough of her friends were in lesbian relationships that she wasn't going to grace the question with a direct answer.

"Does that mean you've had previous relationships?"

"Yes it does, and those are in the past." She practiced what they called the 'most pleasant' smile, as she changed the subject. "I'm sure your viewers are much more interested in the sensational news that NBB is launching a new women's basketball league, the first in recent memory to be broadcast in prime time across the whole season. This will revolutionize the women's game, and give women's sport and basketball fans a completely new viewing experience. I, for one, can't wait."

Clapping resounded in the studio. It appeared they approved of how she'd handled it. The debrief confirmed it, as they watched the video and Arjun reinforced the positives of her approach. "You never looked flustered," he said, "and that's great. You kept smiling – well done – and the transition into the thinking time was pretty fluent. If you keep doing that, you'll do well on screen."

They finished by going over the key points that NBB wanted her to reiterate whenever possible: the new game, a different style, the chance to see the best women in the world, and how happy she was that NBB had taken seriously the public's voice through responding this way to her vid.

She was ready. Or at least as ready as she could be. They gave her an hour to freshen up before donning her chosen outfit. This time it was a smart-casual dress in black and pink and medium-heeled pink shoes. Not her usual look for sure but NBB was running the show. She had to be in make-up by eighteenth hour, where she'd get to watch the announcement. Her first live interview would be with NBB's sports editor, in his usual 15-minute commentary segment immediately after the news. Adie would follow her, maintaining an illusion of independence (just as Danny had thought, Imelda had been working with her behind the scenes to seed ideas and key messages).

She took the time to live-vid her parents. "It's been a crazy week," she started, "but you've gotta make sure you have NBB on from eighteenth hour to nineteen-30. That's when it's happening."

"It?" queried Dad. "You know you still haven't told us what 'it' is."

"You know I can't," she replied, noting the twinkle in his eye through the crystal clear connection. "But you've got good imaginations, and you know where I've been this week, so I think you can figure it out." Her mother nudged Dad out of the way. "Don't worry dear," she said. "We're ready. Got a few friends coming over as well. I've made a huge frittata with our free-range eggs, and the winter veges. One poor chicken gave its life to supply the meat. Then we've got your decadent chocolate mousse for dessert. Wish you could be here."

Danny wished it too, if only for the mousse. It would be made with cream from their five cows, their own eggs, fair-trade chocolate and a dash of orange liqueur. Her mouth watered. "We can save you some if you'll be home soon," Mom said.

"Much as I'd love you to, I don't know exactly when I'll be back. I'm hoping next week but my contract has started so I'm at NBB's beck and call. Anyway. Have a great night and vid me around twenty-third hour if you're still awake. I should be done by then."

They exchanged waves and Dad blew her a kiss before she cut the link. Checking her timeclock, she put through a vid to Vicky. If she was lucky, Nancy would be there for their regular Friday dinner and movie night.

"Hey you," Vic's voice boomed in the quiet room, before the auto-decibel reacted. Nancy's "Hi" came in about the right volume.

"We're here, you're there, tell us when and where, and what we need to hear." Vic's rhyming was right on target.

"I'm here, you're there, NBB news is where, and Canestri's what you'll hear," she replied. "That's all I can say, or they'll take my contract away. I've only had it a day, and I'd like to make hay. While the sun shines," she had to add. Laughter. Two beaming faces. Two excited faces.

"We know, we know, we guessed it right. The big announcement's gonna be tonight. Don't say yes, don't say no, but if we're right, yell ho, ho, ho."

And she did. "Ho. Ho. Ho." Loud and boisterous. Laughing too. "Look. I've got to go, get all gussied up, make-up, hair, the whole works. Make sure you keep watching 'til half past nineteenth hour, OK?"

Two heads nodded. "So we'll have to delay the start of movie night," Vic confirmed, "but we'll be watching something good."

"Let's hope so," Danny said. "Keep your fingers crossed."

"And toes. And everything else," Nancy added. "When will we see you?"

"Probably next week but don't know for sure."

Vicky frowned. "Who's looking after Bumbles? The cat-feeder won't last that long."

"He's at Simeon's. You know, one of the guys I play ball with." Nancy and Vic had met the guys a few times but that part of Danny's life was of no interest to them. Yet, both of them raised their eyebrows with almost identical quizzical expressions.

"Simeon?" Nancy said. "Which one is he? The fat one? The gangly one? The cute blondie or the tall, dark and dreamy one?"

Danny processed their descriptions. Sort of apt she supposed, if you were looking for easy ways to differentiate. "From those descriptions, I'd have to go with the tall, dark one," she said. "We were sorting through all the vid comments and one kind of freaked me out by threatening my cat."

"What?" "What?" The questions rang out only milliseconds apart. "Threatened Bumbles?" said Vic. "That's crazy. Who was it?"

"We don't know. And it was probably just to scare me. And it worked. So Simeon offered to take Bumbles to his place while I'm away. That's where he is until I get back."

"Good move," said Vic. "And I hope you find out who it is. Anyone who threatens an animal should be chemically neutered or isolated." Vic and a couple of her friends took care of stray animals, mostly cats, in her neighborhood, just so they wouldn't be eliminated. She had an agreement with the local Admin to leave the animals alone. If anyone complained, they came to Vic first.

Nancy was on a different track. "Simeon," she said. "How did you come to be going through your vid comments with him?"

"I can't remember. We were talking before the Saturday game and he volunteered to help out. His job involves some kind of analysis and there were 5,000 comments to go through, so I figured I could use the help." Danny felt bad about not telling the whole truth but she didn't want them thinking it was something it wasn't. Or even that it was something. Although that thought made her consider whether it might be. *Did she want it to be? Gaia. Shut up mind. I don't have time for this.*

"Hmmm," said Nancy. "Well that was nice of him to take the pussycat. That's one thing we don't need to worry about."

"Assuming he knows how to take care of a cat," Vic added. "Does he?"

"Sure. And Bumbles seems to like him." Oops. If they pursued that comment, how would she explain that he slept over at her house last week? But they didn't.

"Well, Bumbles is reasonably friendly," Vic concluded.

"Sorry girls. I've got to go. Make up is calling. Check out my outfit – I'll be looking like a super vogue in no time!"

"You wish," they jeered in unison. She sliced out on their laughter and headed to the shower.

THE ANNOUNCEMENT

Emilie was her stylist. *Thank goodness.* They chatted idly through the news section, Danny perking up every time the news anchor announced, 'And tonight we have something big in sports. Stay with us.' As the sports segment neared, the news anchor threw to the sports reporter, saying "So Bryant, what's the big news?" Danny leaned forward, not wanting to miss anything. Luckily Emilie was mostly done. Only a final fuss with her hair was needed just before she went on set.

"Hello, folks. Here's the news you've been waiting for. As you know, NBB is a public broadcaster committed to showing the full diversity of human life. And today, we're announcing something that truly honors that commitment." He paused to smile encouragingly at his audience. "For the first time in recent history, the most popular sport in Terra Altrix for men and women will be shown in all its dimensions. Today, NBB is proud to announce the launch of the inaugural World Women's League of Basketball, starting in six months."

Danny could just imagine the gasps of horror resounding through the Int. And hopefully the cheers. She knew many women's teams in the new league were watching. A surge of joy swept through her and she couldn't help pumping her fist in the air. "Yeah." Then another "yeah", quieter, more of a statement, a confirmation.

The sports reporter continued, explaining the new league structure, with graphics detailing the competition format, and that five teams from Terram Europae, two from Asiae Nationum, three from Terra Americas, and one each from Terra Australia, Continentem Africa, Regionem Indorum and Terra Ludus would be formed to create the 14-team league. Then images of Danny appeared. "And tonight, we have one of the game's living legends, Daniela Bartoli, live to talk about the new league. As many of you know, her vid arguing for recognition of the women's game has gone viral, and NBB has taken notice. With Most Consistent stats of 24 points, 15 assists and

12 rebounds, along with 4 steals in the former international league, she was a star for Canestri Mulier, the current Terra Australia league champions and semi-finalists at last year's World Championships. Even five years later, footage shot this week of her practicing with her old team gives you an idea of her quality." And they showed a 10-second clip of the 3-pointer from yesterday. Clive had made her look pretty good. Her shot mechanics were textbook. She'd have to thank him later. "So keep your eyes peeled. It will be an action-packed basketball season this year. And now back to other news."

Danny turned off. They had given the new league three minutes of prime time news. And it was only five minutes until her live interview. A thud of nausea hit her. Solid. Then fluttering. *Breathe deep,* she reminded herself. Emilie was fussing, placing a strand of hair just there, another just there. "Don't shake your head," she warned. "It's looking perfect right now. Just walk quietly and carefully to the studio." She grinned encouragement. "Bonne chance. Knock 'em dead."

Danny smoothed her dress as she left. Gaia it felt strange to be walking in heels. Ten slow deep breaths got her to the edge of the studio. She squared her shoulders, took one last breath and walked to the guest couch. An unobtrusive pillow at the base of her spine encouraged her to sit upright but leaning slightly forward. She was very close to the sports anchor. She found this the hardest thing to adjust to. The need to sit almost touching so it would appear like a normal distance to viewers. She wasn't against touching – she loved banging bodies on the court – but this felt far too intimate. You could even smell each other's breath. Now she understood why mints were always provided in the green room. The sports editor favored spearmint it appeared. She had gone for strawberry.

She remembered virtually nothing of the interview. It was like a blank space empty of words but full of sensations – nerves, pleasure, surprise at the anchor's positivity. She knew she'd get a chance to watch it later. She did remember seeing herself on screen, in low-spec vid, receiving her Most Consistent award. Shame about the outfit. What looked stylish then was definitely not now. And they replayed the 3-pointer and some more game time from yesterday. That looked a lot better, even the bit where she ended up on her butt taking a charge. Clive had sneaked in the shot of her and Denise hugging, a real moment of connection. She seemed to recall the voice-over said something about the power of sporting friendships but that was it. Of the questions and her answers, she remembered nothing.

Imelda met her as she walked off set and escorted her to one of NBB's interview rooms. "Well done. It couldn't have gone better. Now I've got three interviews set up immediately. Just repeat what you said and everything will be fine."

Danny didn't want to admit she couldn't remember what she'd said but decided to trust in the training – clearly it had worked. The key messages were hers and she believed in them.

Reporters from NBB's main Terra Altrix competitor, from the Terra Ludus station and an English-language Terram Europae channel were all waiting. They all asked variations of the same questions. None of them ventured into 'chummy girls' territory, although she was prepared for it. By the time she was done, it was twenty-first hour. She was buzzing, alight with energy. Her face hurt from smiling (they'd done a lot of practice to get her smile just right, resonating warmth and friendliness without looking fake).

Imelda was again waiting. "Well done again," she said. "That's enough for tonight. You'll need a good night's sleep because tomorrow is likely to be interviews all day. In the meantime, don't answer any emails from journalists or requests for interviews. We'll handle all that, especially since we've announced you'll be heading up our coverage of the new league. But some journos will try to get to you through the back door. Don't respond, even if they are friends. They know they have to come through us."

By now they were at the back door. "Here's your Escort. Be back here at eighth hour tomorrow. Can you find your way?"

Danny nodded yes. "You're sure it went well?"

"Excellent in fact. You did everything we asked. Now we just have to build on that. Good humor by the way. You can keep doing that as well. See you tomorrow."

As abrupt as usual, Imelda rapidly headed towards the stairs. Danny followed the Escort, trying to absorb the moment. Women's basketball on prime time again, a full season televised, and her involved. Unbelievable. Until this moment she hadn't really believed it would happen, had half-wondered if she was in some kind of extended dream sequence. She decided to give herself another pinch. This time on the belly (couldn't have bruises on show). Ouch. It hurt. Must be real. She felt giddy, like dancing down the street, not that it would be possible in these heels. She hadn't even had time to change before Imelda ushered her out the door. Oh well, she had comfy clothes back at the hotel room. And she could dance there without anyone seeing. And there was bandwidth so she'd be able to celebrate with everyone back home. But it was weird to be here alone, on one of the most thrilling nights of her recent life. An Escort wasn't exactly company and she knew no-one in Mountain View outside of NBB. And she was mainly a commodity to them. Someone who could help sell subscriptions, welcome as long as she did what they needed.

Back in the room, face cleansed, wearing sweatpants and a t-shirt, she checked me-mail. Messages from Mom and Dad, Nancy and Vic, Simeon, and Mike. And then her wor-mails. Over 200 and the announcement wasn't even three hours old. A few from people she didn't know. She'd avoid those. Both Dominic and Constantin had written. She'd read them in the morning.

NBB had left champagne and late summer strawberries. From Terra Ludus. She brought a handful to her nose. Sweet, a little tangy, not a hint of preservative. These were fresh. The first one tasted like heaven, an explosion of juice flooding her taste buds. These were a heritage variety. Mom had tried growing them without much success. She ate another, just as slowly, gazing out the window. Treasuring the experience.

Then she projected the vid messages onto the vision wall. Mom and Dad first. They were beaming. And red-cheeked, she noted. Must have been into the sparkling wine themselves, probably Dad's home-made brambleberry version. "Only time for a quick message," Mom's voice rang out. "But we're so proud of you. So proud." Dad's face came next, his head almost projecting out of the screen as he pressed a kiss to the camera lens. "We know how much this means to you. Can't wait to talk to you about it. Vid us as soon as you can." They jointly chorused 'we love you' as the message ended. Next Nancy and Vic. The image showed them dancing around Vic's living room in some mad approximation of a polka. No audio (Vic must be close to running out of bandwidth). Just dancing. Then their faces and high-fives. 'Vid us. Right now," Vic mouthed as the message went dead. At least it cost them nothing when she did the vidding.

Then Mike. He looked astounded. "How could you keep this from me? You sneaky, little ...." Then he threw his head back and roared his pleasure. Swung the vid around to show Con and Dom on the couch. "We can't believe it. How the hell did you do this? Vid us. Now. We need information. Now."

"You'll be lucky," she said to the blank screen. "You can just wait your turn."

Then Simeon. She didn't know why she'd saved his for last. But there he was. On his couch. With a wine glass in hand, toasting her. "Well done," he said. "Very well done. And you were awesome. So smart and funny and beautiful. How did they manage that by the way? Facelift? Botox?" He laughed. "You're almost as gorgeous as the dollies." Still laughing. "Even Bumbles said so." Turning to look down, "Didn't you?" Clearly Bumbles was on his lap or nearby. "He barely recognized you. You did good, girl. Vid me?" It was a question, a request. He wasn't assuming anything, which she kind of liked. But what did that mean? Only one way to find out. She sent the live request, knowing he was the one she wanted to watch a replay of the interviews with.

PR

Her icom pinged at sixth hour. Arjun. She selected audio only. "Rise and shine," he began. "We need you in early. Can you be here in half an hour?"

"Why? I thought I didn't start until eighth hour." She detected a slight whine in her voice. She must be tired. She hadn't slept well or for long. By the time she vidded Simeon, then her parents, and Nancy and Vic, it was twenty-third hour. And she was still too stirred up to easily rest.

"Too much interest. Too much going on. We need to prep you quickly. Pack for a couple of days away. Bring your ball-playing outfit, wear the official polo shirt and pants. Oh, and make sure you've got your day-time look on before you leave the room."

"Slow down," she said. "A few days. Where? Why?"

"Terra Ludus. This afternoon. There's a lot of interest in you, so be ready to be interviewed today. And we've decided to bring all the coaches of the confirmed teams to TL. They'll arrive late tomorrow and you and Sally-Anne will interview them the next day. The men's basketball fraternity wants in and we can't ignore them. So you need to prep for being the interviewer not just the interviewee, although you'll end up being both at different times."

Interviewer. That would be cool. "Didn't we already do the interviewer prep?" she asked.

"Yes, but that was in the studio. This time you'll be in the field. That means no autocue, and much less control. So we want to go over a few things."

"Alright. That makes sense. Do you know what's happening in the evenings? Do I need anything dressy?"

"Good questions. I don't know yet. So bring one of the evening outfits, and matching shoes. And don't forget your night-time and studio make-up kits. Be as quick as possible."

She arrived to find the studio set up, lights blazing and Emilie waiting. "I'm permanently on call," she explained, taking a seat near the back wall, out of the way. "They're prepping for the outside shots first, then studio."

Arjun strode across the room. "Great. Let's get started. Emilie, come here. You can be the coach." Emilie shrugged and walked towards the open space in front of the anchor's desk.

"Right. Daniela. Imagine this is the coach of any of the teams. You have two minutes to think up some questions that you think the audience would like to hear. Then we're shooting. OK?"

The OK sounded more rhetorical than an actual question so she didn't bother answering, just slid into the anchor's chair and started jotting down questions. Can you tell me about the team's reaction to the news of the new league? What effect will an international league have on the women's game? What's your own reaction? How have other people reacted so far? How will the new league affect your recruiting or team selection? Will you need to prepare differently? *I know it's a yes-no question but I want to ask it anyway.* How do you think your team will go in the competition? What's your favorite aspect of the women's game? What do you like about coaching female athletes? Is there anything else you'd like to say?

"Time's up." Arjun was gesturing her to the open space where Emilie was now standing. "Let's see what you remember or know instinctively. Stand where you think you should be in relation to the camera and the coach," he instructed. "We'll only use one to replicate the actual conditions you're likely to be in. And hold the mic where you think it should be. Start with your PTC."

At her quizzical expression, he explained further. "PTC. That's piece to camera. It's part of your intro – 'here we are with …'."

She did as instructed, remembering to stand much closer than she felt comfortable and to explain to Emilie that this was necessary for the camera shots to look normal. Facing the camera, she began. "Here we are with Emilie de Tourney, coach of the Wonderful Makeups, the newest team in the women's league." Half-turning towards Emilie, she continued, "Coach de Tourney, could you please tell us about the team's reaction to the news of the new World Women's League of

Basketball announced last night?" Danny was pleased she remembered to use the full name of the new competition. She continued through her list of questions. Then turned fully back to her camera to do the outro. "And that's all we have time for. Thanks to Coach de Tourney of the Wonderful Makeups, one of the 14 teams in the inaugural World Women's League of Basketball." Unprompted, she activated a basic Sign Off – "I'm Daniela Bartoli for NBB Sport" – basing it on the millions of times she'd heard sports reporters do their thing.

Five measured claps from Arjun. "Well done. They told me you were a journalist and you just showed that. The questions were great. And the intros and outros were OK too. We just need to do some work on your positioning, and how you hold and move the microphone. And a bit of work on how to interrupt or gently indicate it's time to move to the next question."

Emilie wandered back to her chair while Arjun projected the interview and dissected it for Danny. She wasn't engaging enough with the camera. Instead, she was giving too much focus to the coach. And the mic movement between her and the coach wasn't quick enough so the audio volume kept changing. Arjun walked her through the correct positioning. Not too high so as to obscure their faces. Held so their voices moved across the top of the mic rather than into it. Showed her how and when to move it between herself and coach to avoid 'off mic' audio.

"How come we're using this older technology?" Danny asked. "Don't most interviews now use neck mics?"

"Yes they do. But we have to be on the move today. We have a lot of interviews to get through. And you might be in parts of Terra Ludus with limited connectivity so we need something we're sure will capture both audio and vid. We're also going for a kind of nostalgic old school look to the coverage. Basketball old school, as it should be, and all that. Anyway, you're getting the hang of it. And none of it will be going out live, so we can reshoot if absolutely necessary. Basically, I'd rather have it right first time. Hence the practice." And he put her and Emilie back to work, this time focusing on the equipment and her orientation to the camera.

When he was satisfied – and he showed her exactly what was working on the replays of the interviews – it was off to studio makeup with Emilie, ready for the tables to be turned so she could be interviewed.

"You'll be on both sides," Arjun pointed out. "Interviewing for us, and being interviewed by other channels. On the flitter, I'll give you the list. We've got some suggested questions, but the ones you've been asking seem to work well, and it almost always sounds less forced if the interviewer has a hand in deciding what to ask. You'll be interviewed first – we have three Terra Altrix stations, four live Int-radio interviews, and two with Terram Europae broadcast Int shows. Then tomorrow there's a press conference at eleventh hour with you and all the confirmed head coaches. You might also get some questions because we are implying that it was your vid that led to this new venture." At her nod, he continued. "Then from thirteenth to seventeenth hour you and Sally-Anne will do one-on-one interviews with the coaches. OK?"

She nodded again. And wondered which ones she'd be talking to. And asked, "Which ones?"

"Which teams? Canestri Mulier obviously, and Los Angeles, since you live there. Do you speak any other languages?"

"Pretty much monolingual I'm afraid, except for a bit of te reo Māori, which won't be much use for this situation."

"Oh well, we can't have everything," Arjun said. "We'll figure it out. I've got the list on the flitter. Let's get a couple of close-ups of your face to check the makeup." He ignored Emilie's snort of disgust that he would even dare to criticize her work.

Two minutes later, they were on their way to the flitter-port in an NBB-branded, automated self-driving electrix vehicle, her bag beside her on the back seat. The taciturn Clive was already on board the flitter, no friendlier or communicative than before. She thanked him anyway. "Great images last night," she said. "You really showed what basketball can be. I appreciate it."

"Just doing my job," he grunted. But she detected a slight lift in his facial expression. Progress, she decided.

All flight they went over questions, debated options. Arjun made her practice every interaction with a mic in hand. Whether she was speaking to him, Clive or the flit-server, she had to make sure it was in the right place. By the end of the flight, she couldn't take it seriously, and started doing mock interviews with exaggerated movements and ultra-slow voicing. "Sooo, Cliive. Tellll meee. Our vieewerrrs waant tooo know. Whaaat's it liike, shoooting wooomen's baalll?"

Clive finally cracked a smile. "It's sooo slooow, eeeven an amaaateur could keeeep uuup," he replied, waiting to see her reaction.

"Goood thing wee haave youuu thenn," was her sarcastic riposte. "Wee wouldn't waaant tooo aask tooo much of youuuu." Then she ceremoniously laid down the mic in Arjun's lap. "Too much of a good thing can spoil the delivery," she told him. "I want to be fresh not stale."

"Too late for that," Clive joked back, apparently without thinking.

"Feeling more cheery are we?" Danny responded in kind. "That's a turn up for the books." She could see the war on his face. Did he revert to the grumpy façade or give it up and join them? Joining won, as he released a rare smile.

"Fair enough," he said. "Let's get on with it then. Women's basketball here I come."

As they exited the flitter, heading for the Terra Altrix studios, Danny realized she hadn't even had time to check her icom. She didn't even know how many messages were waiting for her. Oh well, she'd have to deal with that later. It didn't seem like there would be any chance for the next few hours. Maybe she'd get a chance to vid Auntie Marama this evening.

WARNING

They finished Saturday at twentieth hour. Arjun left her with instructions to be ready at eighth hour to prepare for the press conference and coach interviews. Clearly there was no such thing as a weekend in Int-TV.

The upside was their accommodation at the Terra Ludus Hilltop. Danny's 45th floor room had a king-bed, a blissful spa pool with jets, and a view over Ākarana citie. Hilltop was in a cluster of high-rise hotels designed for the tourist market. They towered over the generally low-rise, two-storey buildings with their abundant trees and gardens, interspersed with sport stadia of various kinds.

From her window she counted athletics, the main boxing stadium, six kinds of football fields (soccer, American, rugby union, Australian Rules, rugby league and Gaelic) and even a specialized korfball complex. Clive would be salivating over that.

Each building had its use emblazoned in huge organic phosphorescent lights on the roof or sides or etched into its turf, for the edification of the millions of annual visitors and Int-TV viewers.

And there was the new basketball complex, built three years ago on reclaimed land vacated when the Ākarana citie shipping port relocated south to make way for harbor-front stadia, hotels and apartments. She'd been told it was inspired by the old Wimbledon tennis set up, being a mix of higher and lower profile courts, with seating and prices to match. She'd played the women's final five times on the main court in the old stadium. The new complex featured two main courts, each with seating for 50,000. That was where they'd done the pre-launch vid with Canestri Mulier. Then there were seven smaller courts that catered for audiences ranging from 5,000 to 20,000. The plexiglass enclosed edge pods each contained a warm-up court, most open for public viewing from the park-like grounds outside. It was beautiful outside and in. What would it be like to see World Women's League of Basketball blazing from the main dome? Regularly. Weekly.

Even after a long soak, with jets on low massage, she couldn't sleep. So she opened wor-mail to find 800 messages, many of them from people she didn't think she knew. She read the known ones first. Mostly acquaintances and some old teammates congratulating her or expressing support for the new league. Many were enthusiastic about subscribing to the new league. They complimented her on how good she looked on screen. No sarcasm or joking. This was genuinely positive and encouraging but she didn't reply to any, just kept reading.

Halfway down she found one from Mike. A day after his vid, he'd repeated his demands, wanting to know why she hadn't told him earlier and desperately seeking any inside information. She responded, writing that she'd see him next Saturday all going well and suggesting he better get his women's questions into the quiz night before everyone else caught up. That would get him riled up.

She was smiling as she opened the next one, entitled Congratulations. "So smarty pants, you think you're going to get away with it, don't you?" She shivered, and almost closed it down, but the next words drew her on. "I've already warned you once. I know where you are, and if I see you on the Int one more time, I will find you. Basketball is not for women. You can't play, and even being on the court is an embarrassment to the game. The hardwood is where boys become men, where success comes from physical and mental toughness, where fronting up matters. I don't want to see two chicks going tit-to-tit, at least not with their clothes on. It's wrong on too many levels. So this is your second and final warning. Shut it down, shut yourself down or I will do it for you."

It felt the same as the previous message, the one Simeon told her to take to the peacekeepers. But she hadn't. Especially after Imelda dismissed it as unimportant. What should she do now? Everyone would be asleep. And she didn't want them to think she wasn't up to the rigors of her new job. Imelda had warned her it would be rough but that the haters rarely followed through.

Without any apparent volition, she flicked her wrist, and her fingers tapped out a vid request on her bare arm.

"Hey girl. Getting home late from a date?" Simeon's sleepy but jokey opening died quickly as he caught sight of her face. "What is it?"

Even on the less-than-perfect projection onto her skin, she could see his eyes narrow and his body tense, waiting, like a cat stalking a bird.

"It's another message," she started. "Like that first one, the one you wanted me to call the peacekeepers on."

"Send it to me. Now." And she did, taking time to still her trembling fingers so she wouldn't tap the wrong contact. She watched him open it, as he propped himself upright against his bed-head, his mouth tightening and a deep frown appearing as he read further. "Right," he said. "This time you have to notify someone. Right now."

"But it's twenty-second hour here," she protested. "Everyone's asleep."

"So was I," he noted. "But that's not important. I've seen this kind of thing before and multiple threats need follow up."

"But Imelda said…" She got no further before Simeon burst in.

"Prig Imelda. I'm serious Danny. You need to follow up. And if you don't, I'll do it for you. In fact, I will do it for you. I've got some buddies who deal with this kind of thing regularly. I'll run it by them. I've got a copy of the original response to the vid and this one."

She immediately felt lighter. "But…" Again, she wasn't able to finish.

"No buts. You lock your door, put something against it. Have the phone within reach and know which button to push. Do you know anyone nearby? What about that guy Manu?"

"No. And Manu's a couple of hours away."

"That's a pity. In that case, ring hotel reception and tell them you've received a non-specific threat and to call both the peacekeepers and you if anyone suspicious asks for you. OK?"

"You're scaring me," she said.

He immediately and obviously made an effort to relax. "Sorry. It's just that this kind of thing is part of my job. I can't say any more than that, but I do think this is potentially a real threat. Probably not, but possibly. So I'd rather you took precautions you might never need than did nothing. OK?"

She nodded.

"And you can vid me anytime, day or night. OK?"

She nodded again, feeling simultaneously stunned, protected, frightened and happy. Happy was an odd reaction. It was Simeon she realized. *He's got my back.* And that made everything seem alright.

AUTHENTICITY

After a restless sleep she was woken by the morning light-alarm slowly brightening the room until it was impossible to keep her eyes closed pretending it was still night. The chair wedged against the door hadn't moved, and last night felt like an overreaction. Reception hadn't called so clearly nothing untoward had taken place.

She had no idea what to expect today, but Arjun had seemed excited. It was still early so she decided to take a quick jog up to the top of the extinct volcano on whose sides the hotel sat. She pulled on her branded leggings and top, followed by the branded socks and running shoes. *Just a moving billboard* she thought, deciding it was too early and too dark to have to worry about makeup. As her feet paced out the winding single-lane road towards the top – no vehicles allowed – other human-shapes appeared out of the gloom heading in the opposite direction. It was peaceful, the mist dampening sound and vision. *It feels like freedom.* She relaxed, although the slight hitch in her breathing was evidence she needed to do this more regularly. As she cleared the trees into the open area at the top, hints of daybreak appeared, subtle pinks tickling the undersides of the clouds. She didn't have time to linger so returned the same way she had come up, encountering more runners and walkers who had ventured out at sunrise.

She had time for a quick shower and then it was on with the daytime makeup and the NBB-provided interview outfit. This time a form-fitting, knee-length black skirt, thigh-high black boots and a pink silk top paired with a pink and black pashmina designed to accommodate a wide range of temperatures. Arjun met her in the lobby at eighth hour, as promised. She couldn't help looking carefully at everyone there. No-one stood out. It appeared to be mostly business-types, men and women, and some who were obviously tourists, talking loudly in Terra Altrix accents. She couldn't understand why their standard middle-aged tourist outfit never seemed to change – khaki shorts, white polo or t-shirt, white sport socks and sneakers. Clothes and technology had moved on, but the travelling middle-classes continued to embrace this out-dated vision of I'm-on-holiday comfort. Anyway, although many looked out of fashion, none looked out of place. She kept pace with Arjun as he strode towards the basketball complex. Clive wasn't with them. Nor was Sally-Anne.

"So what's the plan?"

"Just you wait and see. Have I got a surprise for you." Arjun was unusually chirpy. "You won't need to do anything this morning but relax and enjoy."

"Enjoy what?"

"Like I said. You'll just have to wait and see."

Five minutes later they were in pod 14, one of the few without a plexiglass viewing window. It was dark inside, lit only by what appeared to be a range of tiny twinkles set into the roof and sides. Arjun handed her a light headset, complete with a tiny earpiece, and gloves. "Put these on and enjoy. We're going to announce this on prime time sport on Friday night. I wanted to give you a sneak preview and get your thoughts on how to promote it."

"Promote what?" She sounded a bit like Ms Super-Questions. But he wasn't giving her much to go on.

"We've done last year's World Championship semis and final for the full immersive experience," he said. "They'll be the first women's basketball games to be broadcast in this format. It will just blow people away."

Blow them away alright. Men's basketball had experimented with it around 2015 but the market was so niche that it wasn't financially viable. The women hadn't even tried because the cost was so exorbitant. But NBB had already done it. Wow. This could be amazing. The closest she'd come to this kind of experience was watching at Mike's, where he'd set up his media room with full surround sound, 3-D technology and a screen that took up one wall, curved one-third of the way round the neighboring ones and projected onto part of the ceiling. They always watched the important games at his house. There was something so real, so almost-there about it.

Full immersion could only be better, especially for last year's final, in which the lead had changed constantly, in a physical battle for dominance that had seen numerous bodies hit the floor, and even a broken nose if she recalled correctly. Arjun talked her through how to shift between choices, using the technology embedded in the fingers of the gloves. *Just like changing guns in Alien Warfields. Easy once you know the gestures.* What viewing location would she choose? The commentator? The ball? No, that would be nauseating. One of the athletes? The coach? Even the basket was an option. She removed her boots – thinking she'd need the stability of her feet on the ground. She experimented in the first half of one semi-final, beginning with the standard wide-angle viewing position and moving closer and closer to the action. Being the ball was truly disorientating so she lasted less than 30 seconds with it, the coach was infuriating, and the standard screen camera position seemed too far from the action, even with close-ups. She settled on the shooting forward for Canestri Mulier, the position she would have played. And it was just like they advertised it. Fully immersive. Just like being there. So close that she could detect individual droplets of her opponent's sweat, so 'there' that she could almost feel her rapid breathing, the physical pain of body contact. She could hear the creative abuse conducted in an undertone designed to be inaudible to the normal microphones. Only those who paying for immersion would have access to this level of audio. And she realized that NBB must have had this in mind for some time because otherwise how could they have captured it. The only disconcerting element was when she unconsciously flinched or moved to intercept a pass, or avoid an opponent, or wanted to pass to an open teammate, and the real player did something else. Rather than the desired embodied experience, it was like being dissected, being in two places at once, moving her own body in real time on the basis of what she saw, only to be visually tripped up (tricked?) by what the actual player did. She decided she was more comfortable with the other forward, whose embodied reactions more closely mirrored the actions Danny would have made in the same situations. But even then, she found herself physically and mentally stranded on more than one occasion. Perhaps this experience would be more coherent for someone who was a watcher. She was too much an athlete, and the experience was too real for her not to react as she would have in a real game.

When the game ended, she felt as physically drained as if she'd played the game herself. But she wasn't covered in sweat and bruises. Her NBB outfit was as pristine as when she left the hotel. Immersion was unlike anything she'd experienced before. But who would be able to afford this experience? What would it do to pull in otherwise ambivalent or neutral viewers?

When she exited the pod, Arjun was waiting, 'uh-oh' written plainly across his face. "Enjoy it?" he said, not really waiting for an answer. "Good. Now something's come up that we need to deal with immediately." His staccato speech was accompanied by his rapid departure from the building. She almost ran to catch up. They were back at NBB studios within minutes. He hustled her into a small viewing booth. "Sit down and watch this," he ordered, remaining standing. On screen she was surprised to see her face – how long ago? 12 years maybe? – and then leaning towards it Adie Supruniak's. A deep belly-laugh escaped. She knew what was coming. Arjun spun towards her in surprise. This response was clearly not what he expected. On screen her lips and Adie's met, interlocked and they exchanged what appeared to be a passionate kiss. Then the screen went blank.

"So?" he said. "Is this real?"

She was still giggling. "Of course it's real. It was a joke. A dare. It was more than 10 years ago for Gaia's sake. Where the hell did you find it?"

"It's all over the Int," he said. "Not so funny for NBB."

"But it is funny. Surely no-one cares about a little kiss these days. Everyone tries it. Adie and I are both hetero anyway. Or at least I am. I know she used to be."

"It appears she is," he said darkly. "And she seems to see it the same way you do. She's already posted a vid response. Watch this."

Adie's face appeared. She did a mock interview with herself, humor lighting her eyes. "So Adie, what do you make of this vid released last night claiming you and Daniela Bartoli are 'chummy girls' who shouldn't be allowed on Int-TV?"

"Well, Adie," she replied to herself, "That's a good question. But an even better one is 'who cares?' As it happens this was a dare in our early days at Canestri Mulier. Everyone drew a dare out of the hat after the team was named. I got this one. And Danny got the other half."

"So, Adie, can you tell us what it was like?"

"Of course, Adie. Not that it's anyone's business but it was nice. Soft, tender, hesitant, sweet. Enough to know that kissing women wasn't for me, or for Danny I think. But harmless fun. Maybe the person who posted the vid should try kissing someone of the same sex for themselves." By now she was laughing aloud. "Signing off."

Danny couldn't stop grinning. Arjun had finally given into a small smile but his voice was serious. "NBB is worried about bad publicity. This vid has gone viral, just like yours did. And the person (probably a man) who posted it is arguing that basketball is full of lesbian women that no right-thinking people would support. You know that's the hidden discourse that we're trying to counteract. That's why we've got you and Sally-Anne and Adie on board. So having you and Adie kissing all over the Int isn't helping us at all. So you're not doing the press conference or any interviews today. We need to control this as much as possible."

"That's ridiculous," she said, waving off his concerns. "It's a storm in a teacup. I'm happy to do a vid response too. I like Adie's approach. Maybe I could call for a rematch just to entice more clicks! Really, it's such a non-issue."

"Not for us. So, for now, you're grounded. But maybe this is the way to go about it. I'll check with Ms Consonati. Humor and not taking it seriously might be an effective counter."

And that's how Danny found herself restricted to her hotel room during the day. She kicked off her shoes, did the requisite face-cleansing, plumped up three pillows and settled down to what Mom and Dad still called 'watching telly between your toes'. A luxury. Only to be engaged in while staying at hotels. Never at home where viewing of any kind was confined to the living areas or perhaps a small screen in the kitchen if it was a separate room. The 50-inch screen was almost as wide as the bed. Perfect for watching basketball. Imelda pinged her while she was in the middle of reading her daily 'Bumbles report', a mix of Bumble's activities and Simeon's summaries of the Int chatter. As usual, Imelda got straight to the point, acknowledging Danny with a nod as she started speaking.

"Good thinking. We've decided that you and Adie are on the right track. So you're both appearing on TL's most popular Int talk show tonight. Adie's on a flitter now. Arjun will pick you up at fifteenth hour. What are your plans for today?"

"Well, since I'm stuck in my room, I'll finish reading my daily summary of Int chatter about the league and watch some basketball, if that's alright with you."

"I understand," she said. "I get it. You're grumpy about our decision. But that's just the way it is. We can't have the press conference derailed. And what was that about a summary? When do you find time to do that? We've got you fully booked."

"They're not mine," she said. "A friend is doing a daily roundup. He's in some kind of analytics and says he enjoys it."

"Send me a copy now and I'll have a look. If I like it, we might want to talk." She sliced out.

Danny swiftly extracted the summary part and pasted it into a message, explaining that it came from Simeon Autlander. She'd already decided Imelda wouldn't appreciate the Bumbles' report.

Her icom pinged again within five minutes.

"This is quality data. Just what we're looking for. We should put him on retainer. Ask him if he's interested. Daily reports at the moment, then others on request. We pay well. Let me know."

"Alright. I'll ask him tonight."

"No. Do it now. Go."

So she did. It was fourteenth hour at home and he was likely to be watching the game or maybe still playing pickup. Where was it being held this week? Mike's? Dominic's? She'd try Mike first. At least he was always Int-connected.

"Oh, so the world celeb has finally deigned to make contact," he ribbed her on opening. "Missing your buddies on a Saturday afternoon, eh? Realized all those sycophants don't really understand you?"

She shook her head. *Idiot.* "Yep. They're all chasing the next best thing and left me all on my lonesome. So I've finally come to my senses. Where are you?"

"Dom's," he said. "DELTS are about to start. Where are you?"

"Terra Ludus. I'll be here all next week and then prepping for a trip to Terram Europae. Is Sim there?"

"I knew it. You don't care about me at all. Don't care that we creamed them on quiz night. Don't care that I'm desperate for new facts for next week. Do you realize the Basketball Hall of Fame has hardly any women's info online. Astounding. What century are we living in? Do you have time to get me something?"

"Me-mail me what you want. I will if I get a chance, but no guarantees. They're keeping me pretty busy but I've got a few hours free today. You can also try Denise you know. Now is Simeon there or not? I've only got a few minutes."

"Don't get on your high horse. I'm just trying to cover my bases. Denise isn't very quick to respond. And Sim's playing pick-up. Should be back in …" He paused, head cocked, clearly listening. "Sounds like they're back. Want to stay on or ping back in a few?"

"I need him now. Can you grab him?" She watched Mike unwillingly hoist himself out of his favorite chair. "OK," he grumbled, "but you owe me. Get me that info."

Sim's sweat-drenched face filled the icom screen. "Hey."

"Hey back. Sorry for interrupting game day but I've got a proposition for you."

"I knew you'd finally see the light," he teased. "Knew you'd never fall for any of those gorgeous buff bodies on TL. I'm willing to consider a proposition now that you're a famous celeb. So lay it on me."

"Bozo," she replied, feeling a blush steal up her cheeks. She would like to proposition him, she realized, and with something quite different than the one she was about to present. "The proposition doesn't come from me," she started.

"Oh. Even better," he joked. "Would it perchance be from thy inestimably beauteous kissing partner Adie Supruniak? I knew she'd be too shy to approach me directly."

"She doesn't even know you," Danny retorted, a hint of vinegar in her tone. "And believe me, shy isn't a word in her vocabulary. And I have to assume you've seen that stupid vid that's doing the rounds.

"Undoubtedly. And a great deal of pleasure it has given us all. We never guessed."

"Stop it now. Be serious. I have an employment proposition for you."

"So Int-TV isn't paying you enough. You've had to turn 'professional'? I hear there's plenty of work on TL."

Now she couldn't help but laugh. "Seriously, Sim. I don't have much time. I showed your latest report to Imelda ..." She didn't get any further before Simeon broke in again.

"I've got it," he said. "She wants to sign Bumbles to a contract. He is a clever cat. Or is it that I'm a clever storyteller. She does realize Bumbles isn't writing the reports doesn't she?" He was clearly enjoying himself. Too much adrenaline and pleasure hormones from the pick-up game, Danny had to assume.

"You won the game didn't you?"

"Of course. Dom and I were dom-i-nant. Why?"

"Because you're unable to concentrate," she replied. "Just like a two-year-old after way too much sugar."

"Ah well. It's not often I get this pleasure. With you away, it's my big chance. And I'm taking it baby!"

"Don't let it go to your head. I'll be back soon and then you're in trouble."

His eyes lit up and smile he gave her was full of genuine pleasure. "Really. Soon?"

"Maybe not soon enough," she mused. "I'm here all next week and then getting ready for a trip Terram Europae to shoot interviews with the new teams. Then I should get a few days at home before trips to interview the other teams. No idea what days of the week though." She realized she had already assumed he'd keep Bumbles again. The tone of his daily reports suggested he was quite enjoying the company. But before she could ask him, he'd already volunteered.

"I suppose that means you'll need me to keep Bumbles safe," he said. "That damn cat is ruining my life. Can't stay out all night because he gets lonely and tips over the bathroom trash bin. Are you sure you didn't make up that threat yourself just to suck me into this?" He was still smiling.

"Sure. What else do I have to do with my time than try to sucker people into cat-sitting for me? And you fell for it, hook, line and sinker. And now you're lost because Bumbles has worked his secret kitty magic on you."

"That he has," Simeon conceded. "I'm happy to keep him company. He seems to have settled in quite well."

"If you feed him, pet him, and let him sleep with you, he's completely happy." She could see from Simeon's guilty look that Bumbles had already inveigled his way into his bed. "Hah. You're letting him on the bed aren't you?" A nod. "In the bed?" Another nod. "You're a goner then. He knows he's the boss now. Good luck exerting any authority. But, seriously, are you OK to keep him for another few weeks? Things are sure to calm down soon."

"Happy to keep him. And you should probably stay over when you get back as well. That threat is still out there, even though we're still trying to track it." Then he rushed on. "Now, what did you really vid me for?" Down to business.

Still processing the 'still trying to track it,' comment, she tried to focus. "As I tried to say before, I showed Imelda your daily summary and she's really impressed. She wants to retain you as a consultant or something. Daily reports for the next couple of weeks, then upon request. Says they pay well."

"I'm already paid well," was his first response. "But a bit of extra e-cash wouldn't go astray. Might keep the cat in fresh meat at least."

"Fresh meat?" She fed Bumbles fairly basic biscuits and tinned cat food, all she could afford on her unreliable income.

Simeon had the grace to look slightly ashamed. "Well, after you left he was a bit down so I thought he might need some treats to help him settle, so I shared some of my steak before I cooked it, and he was so funny, growling at it like it was alive, that I gave him some more. He seemed to like it so much that I kept doing it. So we've had steak for dinner every night this week."

"You didn't tell me that. And you don't need to do that. He's perfectly alright on cat biscuits."

"Um," Simeon was biting his lip. "Actually, he won't touch them. He just looks at them in disgust and starts howling." He continued rapidly before Danny could say anything. "So tell Imelda the answer is yes. I need the funds to keep the cat in fresh meat. I'll send you the whole Bumbles report and just give them the media summary part. Is that OK?"

"Fine with me. But you're in trouble if he won't eat biscuits when I get him back. My salary doesn't stretch to daily steaks." She smiled in case he thought it was a serious threat. "I'll give Imelda your details so she can get in touch, alright?"

"Sure," he said. "But not in the next two hours. DELTS are about to play. You better get in front of a broadcast. I expect a full analysis after the game."

"Probably by me-mail," she said. "Unless you want to Int-chat through the game. I'm more-or-less free during the game but no live-vid access, except for official business."

"Let's do that then," he said. "Chat me when you're open."

She sent his details to Imelda, then pinged her and asked to be excused so she would watch the game.

"So you really are a basketball fan," Imelda mused.

"Of course. Why else would I have made the vid, and agreed to all this?"

"Perhaps you were making a feminist statement?"

"Not really. It's more about equality. There's no earthly reason why men's basketball should get all the attention, glory, money and media, when the women put in just as much work and play just as well. That's my point."

DOWNTIME

As she settled in to watch the DELTS, she realized she could perhaps have gotten tickets to see them live. Quite bizarre to know the game was going on just below her. Why hadn't she thought of it? She'd have to talk to Imelda. Maybe she could sell it as another form of promotion. She, the micro-celeb, showing support for the (inferior, hah, hah) men's game by attending live matches. *Note to self: check with Arjun about next week's schedule.* If she was still in TL next Sunday, especially if the DELTS made it through to the play-offs, she should be at the game. Maybe she could score tickets for the guys. Sell that as well – Daniela Bartoli and her crew. A pity none of them had made the NBA or Basketball Association International league, although Sim and Dom both had trials. Perhaps Manu too if he's around. He had a good profile in TL and maybe he could use it to promote waka ama. *No. Stop thinking like that. They're friends, not promotional tools.* Gaia. She was starting to sound like Imelda.

They Int-chatted through the game – she missed the first 10 minutes – alternating between abuse and informed critique. The new center had been the key to maximizing the team's capacities. The DELTS had their weaknesses still, but enough all-round firepower to keep their opponents in check. And they won again. By only 3 points but enough to go through to the semis. She made sure to ask what they were all doing next Saturday. Con's was the site and they'd all be there. *Good. If I can get tickets, they should all be available. Maybe I can talk Imelda into flights as well. NBB's flitter will fit them all if it's free. Especially if it's coming here anyway. Maybe I could do some celebrity interviews at the game, get myself interviewed at half-time? It would be worth it to get the guys to a game.*

Right after the game ended, she made a quick vid and sent it to Arjun. Pitching the ideas. They'd talk in the morning. She skimmed her wor-mail. Nothing out of the ordinary, and nothing that seemed urgent enough to read in detail or respond to. She watched the press conference, noting which of the coaches spoke decent English and who needed translators. She tried to memorize their faces so she'd recognize them later.

Then Arjun was at the door, carrying a long garment bag.

"How may I help you sir?" she couldn't help saying as he offered it to her. "Would you be needing a tip for your services?"

He just shook his head with a wry grimace, clearly not impressed by her attempt at humor. "It's your dress and shoes for this evening. Special delivery to increase the wow factor, according to Ms Consonati. Over to you, and no need for makeup, they'll do it at the studio, but you've only got about twenty minutes."

Danny made the deadline, with her evening makeup already applied. She didn't know any of the TL makeup people and didn't want to let Emilie down. Arjun whisked her to the studio, where she soon found herself giggling in the grey-walled, utilitarian 'green room' with Adie and a bottle of champagne. They had no plans to drink too much alcohol, just enough to dampen their nerves and take the edge off.

It wasn't every day – in fact it was never until now – that she would be kissing another woman live in front of the whole world. The wardrobe and makeup crew had completed the finishing touches. Danny's dress was floating layers of filmy silk in various shades of green, flaring out from the waist to settle at her ankles. Adie's already blonde actress looks were enhanced and they'd further played up Danny's olive skin, dark hair and eyes. They looked like opposite sides of the same coin (if you ignored the obvious height differences, and long wavy versus straight short hair). Day and night, some might say, sunshine and moonshine. That got them giggling some more. The Int clicker along the bottom of the screen showed record viewing numbers, which just kept growing as their appearance neared. "It's crazy isn't it?" said Adie. "That a little kiss would galvanize people this way. I guess we better give them what they want."

As Adie headed down the hallway to the set – her boisterous stride at odds with the glittery lavender-blue sheath dress and high heels – she turned to remind Danny "and don't forget to promote the World Women's League of Basketball. That's why we're here. Let's turn the whole idea of chummy girls on its head." Adie's steps shortened as her stride became a sexy glide across the stage. Feeling somewhat like an elephant following a gazelle, Danny did her best to imitate the smooth walk. Adie embraced the male host, Fa'amalua Latua, with a feminine giggle and a kiss on the cheek. She patted his face, saying in a loud stage whisper, "No. No. No kiss on the lips for you my friend. I'm saving myself for Daniela." Danny confined herself to shaking his hand. They sat side-by-side on the standard guest couch as the host recapped the story to date.

"Well viewers, here we are with the two most trending (and fashionable I might add) women on the Int: ex-basketballers-turned-broadcasters Adie Supruniak and Daniela Bartoli. As you all know, someone anonymously posted a vid of them kissing on a dare over 10 years ago, complaining that women's basketball was full of chummy girls and should be avoided at all costs. This individual also criticized NBB's launch of the new World Women's League of Basketball for the same reason. So, Adie, to you first, what's your response?

"Well, Fa'amalua, it just made me laugh out loud. Who on earth, or Mars for that matter, cares about some ancient piece of vid of two girls kissing? That's so passé, so twentieth century. Almost everyone I know has kissed someone of the same sex, for fun, for a dare, or just to see. And women basketballers are no more or no less likely than anyone else to engage in a little experimentation."

The host turned to Danny. "And your thoughts Daniela?"

"I have to agree with Adie," she said. "If this person's intent was to shame us or shame NBB, it has totally backfired. We were new to the team, and we had the luck (or misfortune)," she laughed wryly, "to pull each other's names out of the hat. It was a two second kiss, on a dare. No-one took it seriously at the time, and I don't see why anyone should now. Although I have to say we have stayed very good friends." At her overemphasis on 'very good' the host's broad smile grew broader.

"And you're about to prove that to us tonight I hear," he said.

"Of course," they replied in almost perfect unison. Adie continued, "We're not ashamed. We are both hetero, not that it matters, and we wanted to show that a kiss doth not a lesbian make."

"Not that we're against women kissing women," Danny continued. "Love and friendship are what matters. Love you who love, and cherish your friends, even if means kissing them live in front of the world." Again her response brought a smile from the host and outright laughter from the studio audience.

Buoyed by the champagne, Danny turned to the audience, and simultaneously stared straight into the camera lens. "Ready everyone? Here's what you've been waiting for. We, Daniela Bartoli and Adie Supruniak, officially launch the World Women's League of Basketball, the feminine basketball league, with a kiss."

They had fun with it, moving towards each other slowly to give the seven cameras (*7 for Gaia's sake!*) ample time for close-ups, then ever so gently touching their lips, before raising their hands to cup each other's faces and produce a mock-impassioned lip-lock. They parted, slowly again, and turned to the audience. Together they took a bow to thunderous and supportive applause, before walking off set before the host could ask any more questions. They giggled their way back to the green room where Arjun waited, looking slightly stunned. "That was ... impressive," he finally managed. "Very authentic."

"Of course it was authentic," Adie said. "We're professionals. We don't do anything half-assed. We gave them what they wanted, shut up the idiot who posted the vid, and promoted the league to thousands of potential subscribers and ... prig." She was laughing again. "Prig. Prig. Prig. I forgot to say 'And don't forget, women can do anything'. That was going to be my exit line. Oh well, plenty of time for that when all the post-kiss interview requests come in."

"What?" Danny thought this would be the end of it.

"Oh, you little media innocent," Adie mocked her. "You thought this would shut people up. No way. It's just going to get them talking even more. So it's up to us to use that to promote the league. I've got some ideas. And don't steal my exit line. You'll have to come up with your own wordsmithery."

Danny was silent for a few moments. "I've got it. 'And you think the SportLive kiss was something. Wait 'til you see women's basketball in full-immersion'. NBB is launching full-immersion women's ball this week, with a replay of last year's first semifinal, so we've got to find a way to promo that too. What do you think?" She was looking at Arjun.

"It could work," he mused. "We've got the release vid almost ready to go. I forgot to tell you we were filming you watching the immersion Danny, so there's some entertaining splicing of you going one way and the actual athlete going the other. We need to put some words around it. Seed it humorously I think, something about there's more than one way to play."

"That's it," Adie jumped in. "More than one way to play. That's my tagline. Yeah. It works on so many levels." She pumped her left hand in the air, then grabbed the remains of the champagne and poured it into their glasses. "A toast to 'more than one way to play'." And they raised their glasses. Three voices in unison. "More than one way to play." But Adie didn't get to use it. NBB pumped it out within two hours, before Adie's daily commentary show. Imelda's vid incorrectly congratulated Danny for coming up with it. "Great idea. Plays to our argument that women's ball is a different kind of ball. Gives a subtle nod to the lesbian audience, and highlights the idea that sexuality is fluid. I didn't think the whole live kiss thing would work, but LiveSports' numbers are off the charts and it's translating into hits on the League website, a lot of them from men who also click on mainstream sports sites. You and Adie have a good feel for the sport audience. Well done. Keep it up."

MORE SUPPORT

"Great idea," was Arjun's greeting the next morning, as she met him for breakfast. "Ms Consonati thinks having you and your basketball friends at the men's game will work. She wants you to raise it with Basketball Association International CEO when you interview him today. We'd need their permission to get a camera in there or to upload vid from theirs."

"She went for it? She really thinks they'll go for it?"

"So it seems. She trusts your judgment." Arjun shrugged. "All your instincts have been right so far."

Danny tucked into her bacon and eggs, a smile tugging at the sides of her mouth. The guys would owe her big time. Then she frowned a little.

"What's up?"

"Just thinking about how I can surprise the guys, how to get them halfway here before they figure out what's going on."

"Why would you want to do that?"

"Don't you know anything about one-upmanship?" Shaking her head in mock dismay. "They are gonna owe me so bad for this. There's no way I'm not exploiting its full potential."

Arjun shook his head back at her, his expression indicating *kids these days.*

"You don't have friends like this then?"

"No. And I'm not sure I'd want them either."

"Don't worry. You'll like them. Now give me some peace and quiet to figure this out." Arjun just shook his head again and drained his coffee before heading out of the hotel restaurant.

"Be back here at tenth hour," he said. "Usual interviewer outfit."

She nodded and went back to finishing her breakfast. How was she going to do this? She'd have to get one of the guys involved. But who? Certainly not Dom or Con. Neither of them could keep a secret. Simeon? No. She'd asked so much of him already that she wanted to make sure he fully enjoyed the surprise. That left Mike. He would do it. And he owed her already for the quiz-night win. Right. Give him a call as soon as the CEO gave the go-ahead. They'd come up with some kind of cover story the guys would believe. This was going to be fun.

She spent much of the day with the men's league officials. Her last interview was with the BAI CEO, a surprising supporter. Off camera he said he couldn't see anything but positives, as long as broadcasting the women didn't mean a reduction in men's coverage or a loss of sponsors or advertising money. "Tell them they need to target different companies," he said, "and I'll support the league. Give you good sound-bites." And he did. "Basketball is basketball," he said to camera. "The most popular game on the planet. Men's and women's are two faces of the same game. The men's game is vertical and spectacular. The women's is horizontal and thoughtful. There's room for both in the current market." Not exactly high praise, Danny thought, but innocuous enough not to annoy the hard-core men's fans. And it was better than the other options of silence or antagonism.

And he agreed to let NBB bring a camera to a DELTS game. "I'll organize six tickets in the corporate suite," he said. "And get a spot for your camera guy," nodding towards Clive who shrugged his assent. "Do you want to catch both semis? I'm sure we can get you in sometime soon." He flicked his wrist to check availability, the options projecting onto the sleeve of his white shirt. *No wonder he wears white. It gives a good vid image.*

This was much more than Danny had expected. "That would be amazing if they can get here in time," she said. "And I really appreciate the corporate suite offer. But is there any chance we could be in with the crowd, down near the court? Five of us are really big DELTS fans and this is the first time they've made the semis in years. I think the guys would really want to soak up the atmosphere."

"If you're willing to wait another week, it shouldn't be a problem, at least for the DELTAN game. You might be in the box for first semi. Will that work?" At her nod, he continued, "We'd like to interview you at half-time in exchange, focus on your being a fan."

"That would be great. As long as you don't mind if I give a bit of a plug for the women's league."

"We expect that. Quid pro quo is how it works. But make it clear you're there as a men's basketball fan. Any of your companions worth interviewing as well? Can any of them play?"

"Manu Paraone is a world champion waka ama paddler," she said. When the name didn't generate any recognition, she continued. "He's a native Terra Ludan and a bit of a celebrity over here. And two of the guys had BAI trials about 10 years ago and we play pick up together every weekend."

"Send me their names and I'll check it out with our Comms people. Might select one of them for the half-time three-point shoot out."

"Wow. That would be really great. A couple of them are pretty good from beyond the line." She realized she was reacting like a kid in a candy store, not a professional broadcaster, but she couldn't help it. This was an unbelievable opportunity, a dream come true.

They finished the interview on good terms. As she got ready to leave, he reiterated his message. "Tell the WWLB they can't target our sponsors. If they do, all bets are off. If we lose sponsors, we'll do everything we can to bury you. Right now, we're playing nice. But we don't have to. Do you understand?"

She indicated yes, sneaking a sideways glance at Clive, who gave an almost imperceptible nod and a show of the red light on the camera, held apparently idle at his side. In operation. Still recording. "I'll make sure they hear your concerns," she said, a slight sarcastic emphasis on concerns. "But I'm not the WWLB. You might want to talk to them directly."

"No," he replied, shaking his head. "I can't and won't do that. Our hard-core fans wouldn't tolerate it. So it's up to you. It's on you."

She shook her head. "It's not on me." She really wanted to add, 'and I don't like being threatened' but the relationship was too important to jeopardize. "But I'll tell them what you've said."

They shook hands, him vigorously, her with little enthusiasm, and departed. She beamed at Clive in the lifter and he gave her a wink. The red light was off now but they both knew the lifter could have video or audio recording and that they weren't safe until they were on the street. Anything Clive tried to send within the building was subject to capture by the men's league. So it would have to wait. She made what she thought was innocuous conversation just in case. "So, Clive," she said, "are you happy with the images? You got what you needed?"

"Yes," he said. "Both you and the CEO looked good. The lighting was fine and I managed to frame the view from his office over the basketball complex very well. Audio was pretty much perfect. So I'm pleased. I think NBB will run a good segment from it."

"Excellent," she said. "What's next?"

"We're off to interview a couple of men, ex-professional players," he said. "They're both in support of the new league." The lifter stopped and they exited the lobby as rapidly as possible without looking like they were rushing.

Imelda and Arjun separately congratulated her on keeping her cool and getting the extra audio. "It was Clive who should be thanked," she said, not wanting to take credit. All she did was not mess it up.

"Sure, sure," was Imelda's dismissive response as she moved onto the more important point. "This is very useful to have in our back pocket. We need at least their tacit support at the moment. And I won't hesitate to use it if I have to."

Danny could believe that. Imelda's focus on the success of NBB, and this new league, was ferocious. She could easily believe Imelda would do virtually anything to make sure that NBB profited from her pet project. With someone like her in their corner, it was hard to imagine anything but a successful outcome.

The interviews (minus the threat) aired during the seventeenth hour sports news. The male athletes had been positive. Both had been forced out of the men's league unwillingly and their former unquestioning support for it had disappeared. They weren't directly critical but there was enough between the lines. Kiwane Shallcrass had married a former women's basketball ludio and was now a badged women's referee. So he had some authority to discuss the differences in the games. Danny enjoyed doing the interviews, thinking that the more men they could get speaking in support the better. The interviews were edited to reinforce the More Than One Way To Play tagline.

She watched them from the bathtub, soaking away the lingering after effects of a fast jog up Maungatui. She'd taken the afternoon run after realizing how tight she was. Stretching, she had identified a range of tensions in her shoulders and neck. Even her quadriceps and hamstrings felt stiff, unused. Which was true. She'd been alternately trapped in high heels or sitting or standing around waiting for interviews, with only the immersive experience, a few short walks, and yesterday's morning jog involving anything physical. She needed to move. She couldn't let her fitness slip.

It had been cooling off as evening descended but it would still be light until eighteenth hour. Donning her official tracksuit, she had walked rapidly through the hotel precinct towards Maungatui, the closest of the volcanic cones that dominated the citie. It was her favorite of the two nearby extinct volcanoes, the rise slightly longer but less steep, with views that swept 360 degrees across the city.

At the base, she set her fitness app to record speed, steps, respiration and heart-rate. She jogged the entire base first to warm up. City streets but wide grass verges, recently mowed, just perfect for runners and walkers. And there were plenty about. All ages, she noted, from young kids riding bikes along the sidewalk, keeping pace with a parent, to elderly couples out for an evening stroll. Runners outnumbered walkers. Running styles were as varied as fashions. Her former teammates' descriptions echoed in her head as she passed people: 'praying mantis' – a young woman running with her arms so tightly bent that they looked half the size of normal; roly-poly – a middle-aged guy with a prominent belly and a form of pronation that rolled his gait from side to side; studly – for a well-muscled young man in a sleeveless tank top; enduro for a long-distance runner whose muscle striations and lean frame revealed virtually no body-fat; thudder for the numerous heavy-footed casual runners she could hear long before she saw them. *Shut up. These are real people, doing their best. And you're not perfect either.* She wasn't sure if the last comment was directed at them – the superior ex-teammates – or herself.

Many people nodded as they passed in the opposite direction. *Friendly lot. Not like back in Los Angeles or Mountain View.* Two young girls walked towards her giggling and pointing in her direction. She half-turned to see what was attracting their interest. No-one behind her. Then it clicked. They were looking at her. One gave a hesitant wave as they passed. She smiled back. Heard more giggling behind her. She began to pay attention to people's expressions as they came towards her. The small hesitation in the gait of those who recognized her. The nod of the head or gaze sliding away. A casual 'hi' from a few. A daring 'hi Daniela, give us a kiss,' from a walker in his late teens, accompanied by nudges and guffaws from his mates. "You'd be lucky," she retorted without thinking, which led to outright derisive jeering directed at the young man. Oops. She better think about this.

She plastered a smile on her face, as she faced the steepest part of the climb. Made eye contact and acknowledged every person even though she was feeling the pain of the long, slow uphill. This was only a sliver of a taste of what celebrities faced on a daily basis. But she didn't like it. When she ran, she liked to be inside herself, focused on the embodied sensations, assessing and adapting pace and breathing by feel. She always recorded the measurables but they played no part in her actual run. She decided her pace on how her body felt, how it reacted to the conditions. She'd learned over the years to pay attention, to assess, for example, whether that small burn in her left Achilles meant stop, stretch or run through it. She always enjoyed the view but usually paid little or no attention to who was around her. That might have to change.

At the top, she did three sets of quick runs up and down the 15 steps to the viewing platform. Then moved across to 1950s-style steel balustrades, against which she braced herself for stretching. Funny how even architectural fashions came and went. This one seemed to return every second generation. But she knew that this particular style had never been changed on Maungatui, each Admin deciding to replace rather than update or revise. It gave the place a sense of continuity. It meant that people like her Dad could return and find familiarity, even as the citie changed dramatically around the mountains. She completed one set of stretches on each side, taking in the 360-degree views, including both harbors and the small offshore islands, entranced by the light glinting off waves that smoothed into a single sheet of gunmetal grey. So different from the light on her dawn jog. There was quite possibly nowhere more beautiful on earth, something she hadn't appreciated in her professional playing days.

The platform was filling up with people and she became aware of whispers all around her. Finally someone approached, a woman about 35. "Are you Daniela Bartoli?" Danny nodded and smiled encouragingly.

"Hi. I'm Sandy Ismari. I just wanted to say that what you're doing is great. My husband and I are right with you. Our daughter plays. We both think men's basketball has been dominant for too long. And don't worry about what other people are saying. There are a lot of us who think like you do."

"Thanks very much." Danny extended her arm in an offer to shake hands. It was accepted. "We're doing our best. I hope you'll considering buying a subscription because that's what will make the real difference." Others had begun to edge closer as the conversation continued. Danny began to feel crowded. She turned to face the group.

"Kia ora koutou. Hi everyone. I hope you're enjoying your day. And I hope you'll support the World Women's League of Basketball. Right now I need to finish my run. Got to stay fit for the cameras, and in case one of the teams wants to draft me." In response to her tone, a ripple of laughter ran through the group, which now comprised about 30 people.

One young woman asked, "Could I have a pic with you?" Plastering the smile back on, Danny acquiesced. "Yes. Sure." She stretched her arms above her head, using the move to wipe droplets of sweat from her face, and ran her fingers through her hair. None of the grooming advice had covered what to do if she was accosted during exercise. She asked to see the first images just to check. Her hair looked OK, just needing a quick pull of some flyaway bits of fringe to one side. She spent the next 15 minutes having her image taken with anyone who wanted it. She knew the pix would be immediately flying through cyberspace to every Int platform and social networking site. She placed herself so the WWLB logo was clearly visible in each and every one. Once back at the hotel, she would contact Arjun for advice. She wasn't going to give up running.

The jog back was uneventful. It was dusk and fewer people seemed to recognize her. She breathed deeply, inhaling the coolness, wafts of a highly scented plant punctuating the air. After her bath, she ordered room service and checked a few of the major sites. Yes. The photos were already up. She wor-mailed Arjun and Emilie, asking what to do for next time.

Then she pinged Manu, hoping that bringing him to the game might make up for the fact she still hadn't had time to visit the whānau or Moana who was only days away from giving birth to her third child. He was not only happy to come but willing to be interviewed if asked.

"He rawe rawa atu," was his upbeat initial response. "Bet you don't know what that means."

"Actually, I do," she said. "It's one of my favorite phrases." And she didn't say anything more.

"Well? Do tell."

"Are you sure you know what it means?" she retorted.

"Hah. You don't know. I knew it," he crowed.

"Kāore e hoa. You're so wrong. I do know. It means awesome!"

"Ae. You win. And yes it is. To see basketball played live, courtside! There's no way I can afford that. This will be truly awesome."

"Great. Now you can't tell anyone. It can't get back to Terra Altrix and the guys. It's a surprise for them. And a big score for me."

"I get you. You'll definitely score major points for this. Ka kite a Rātapu."

"Ae. And send aroha to all the whānau from me, especially Moana."

"Ae. Will do," and he waved as he sliced out.

Muscles protesting slightly, she ran again the next morning through the pre-dawn glistening streets, mostly absent of electrix or people, towards the base of another nearby extinct volcano. Maungatahi was smaller but still a good challenge. And she'd read that local volunteers had spent the last decade beautifying what had been citie-owned and neglected land. Now that it had been returned to the original Māori kaitiaki or caretakers, native trees flourished, including manuka, totara, kauri and the architecturally striking cabbage tree, interspersed with nikau palms with their long fronds and spiky, coral-like seed pods. There were other things she couldn't name. Lillies and scented plants that clearly relished the shade. In the open areas, she was greeted by hip-height daisies, their white petals and yellow centers turned towards the rising sun. Swathes of tiny mountain daisies cascaded down a section of hill, displacing grass and weeds in a colorful display of white and red. It was like being in another world, the noises of the citie disappearing into birdsong.

The descent was fast and the transition back to citie life sudden. Gone were the real birds, replaced by the dull hum of wheels turning on the throughway and the hoots of electrix cars. Ākarana citie had the ruru or morepork owl as its pedestrian-alert. *The wonders of progress.* Electric cars were so quiet nowadays that the manufacturers had to insert noises to make sure peds didn't get run over. Each region chose its own sound. It could be anything that was unlike the natural auditory input in that area. In fact, the ped-alert was usually the most controversial issue in elections. Making the wrong choice had brought down mayors and councilors around the world. It could be disconcerting to visit new places. She recalled her first visit to Mountain View, with its shivering oak leaf rustling. It felt wrong to hear the effect of wind but not feel it on her skin. She liked Los Angeles. After robust debate, and deeply influenced by the dominant Hispanic community, the citie had decided on a muted pan flute, and with such a wide variety of musical selections that it was never boring.

Over breakfast, she managed to reach Mike at work before his lunch break.

"Hey," she started, as his face appeared on screen.

"Oooh, the famous celebrity has deigned to talk to a pleb. To what do I owe this honor?"

"Well, Mikey," using the nickname that drove him crazy, "I have some information just for you. Can you keep a secret?"

His hesitation showed he couldn't decide whether to respond grumpily to the nickname or to the temptation of new information. Temptation won but he wasn't going to fully concede.

"Depends what it is," was his opening bid.

"Something that will blow your business socks right off," she said. "But you have to agree not to tell anyone, and I mean anyone."

"You can't ask me that," he whined a little. "What if it's good for quiz night? What's in it for me?"

She mulled over how much to say before she gained his full agreement. She was determined that it would be a complete surprise to the other guys.

"Oh come on, you big baby. This is big, big, big and you won't regret it. It's no use for quiz night but there's definitely something in it for you. Come on. Just agree. I don't have all morning. And I'm not going to tell you until you swear you won't tell anyone."

More hesitation but not for long.

"OK. You win. What is it?" Excitement lit up his face and voice as he stood up. "Hold on a min. Just let me find somewhere more private." Then her view was limited to a close-up of material as he concealed the icom against his leg while he moved location. She knew enough to stay quiet. His company wasn't much for private conversations. Once he stopped and returned her view to horizontal, two toilet stalls became visible behind Mike's face.

"So what is it?" he demanded. "What's important enough to vid me at work?"

"I need your help," she said. "You won't believe this, but I've scored tickets for all of us to watch the DELTS play live in two weeks! Amazing huh?"

"Whaaa ...what?" was all Mike could expel.

"Breathe, Mikey, breathe. It's true. I pitched the idea to NBB and they went for it. So they're willing to flit you four over here next Saturday for Game 2 of the semi-final series, put you up in a hotel for the night and get you back for Sunday evening. All you have to do is bring some dress clothes, wear your DELTS gear and maybe take part in the half-time shoot-out.

"Whaaa?" Mike still didn't seem able to speak clearly.

"C'mon Mike. Snap out of it. This is good. Isn't it?"

"Yeah. Yes. Yeah. Of course. Yeah." Then he propped the icom up against the washbasin mirror and started jumping around the cramped space. "Yeah, yeah, yeah," he began singing to an old Beatles tune. "Yeah, yeah yeah. Oh I can't wait to tell the guys."

"But you can't," she interrupted. "That's the deal."

"But how am I going to get them ready?"

"I've thought of that, I think. You need a story they'll believe about something they'll want to do. What do you think about this? When's the next quiz night or the last one? And were any of them on the team that night?"

"Last one was two weeks ago and, no, they weren't there."

"Alright. Does the bar ever hold random draws for things?

"Yeah. Sometimes." A gleam in his eye. "I think I see where you're going. I'll say I've won tickets to the DELTS live in a draw and am taking them with me." He pumped his fist.

"No. It won't work. You have to come up with something else so they won't know what's going on until they're on the flitter in Mountain View or maybe until they land. Oh, and we've got tickets to both games."

"Both games? A flitter? Gaia. This is incredible."

"I know," she giggled. "I can't actually believe it."

"OK. When would we need to be at the flitterport? How long is the flight?"

"A bit under three hours. Yeah, I know," she said in response to his wide-eyed stare. "Hard to believe you can get that far in such a short time. That's what Mach 6 will do for you. But it's a bit scary really. If anything goes wrong, we're toast, literally and figuratively. But, hey, you only live once right? Anyway, the first game starts at seventeenth hour your time on Saturday. You'd have to be at the Mountain View flitterport by thirteenth hour at the latest. So that means the tenth hour zoomer. I'll make sure an Escort is waiting."

"OK. How about this? I'll say I've won a free lunch and overnight stay for four at that new super-tech hotel in Mountain View. What's it called? You know, the one with the 5-star restaurant that everyone's raving about. The one you have to book a year in advance. And that I named them as my companions when I entered the draw, so I have to take them all or forfeit the prize. What do you think?"

"Impressive. It'll work as long as they think they'll be able to see the games. The DELTS are playing second so telling them the prize is the first sitting for lunch will explain the early zoomer, and you'll be finished in plenty of time for the DELTS game. Doesn't that hotel have some special media room as well?"

"Yeah. You're right. I'll check it out. That'll be the clincher. OK. I better get back to work. I'll tell them I ate something last night that disagreed with me and make a couple more bathroom visits!" He laughed aloud at the disgusted look on her face and sliced out.

Simeon's summary came from Bumbles. 'Dear Cat-Mother,' it read. 'Last night was most satisfactory. I had fresh guinea fowl breast for dinner and allowed Simeon to share. He braised his in plum sauce. Each to his own. I growled mine into submission, something he should consider. He stabbed his with a knife and fork. Then he submitted to my desire to curl up on his lap and sleep. As befitting my importance, he carried me to bed, where we spent a pleasant night. I allowed him half the bed. I've ordered him to make the rest of the report himself as it's time for my morning nap. Meows, Bumbles.'

The second half was the summary, more formal, given that other people would see it. 'The bifurcated reactions continue (60% against, 25% for and 15% loosely in the middle) but now most of the attacks are turned on the men. The BAI CEO and Shallcrass received a number of similarly negative and threatening public responses.' Simeon highlighted one, writing, 'It has the same structure as earlier ones sent to Daniela'. The report concluded, 'Both Shallcrass and the other former player are widely dismissed as weak sissies who couldn't hack the rigors of the real game so their views are not worth considering. The attacks on them follow expected norms, with the men feminized in an attempt to deny their views as legitimate. The public negativity continues but is not necessarily representative. People don't always speak or write in support because they fear retaliation or public attack. The overall negative tone of the public exchange to date makes it less likely that supporters will engage online. I see nothing here, other than the highlighted threat to the men's league CEO and Shallcrass that should concern NBB. In fact the finding that a quarter of Int-chatter is not only strongly positive but often actively contesting the naysayers is indicative of a much larger support base. Quote of the day: "If you want us to watch chicks with balls, at least put them in bikinis or lingerie. Football did it. Tennis did it. Do that and I might, just might, consider it".' Simeon finished in his own words, suggesting that she take care of herself, and advising her to alert the BAI CEO and Shallcrass to the threat. No mention of the trip to Mountain View. Obviously Mike hadn't contacted him yet. As for the threat, she decided not to do anything immediately. NBB could alert them if they thought it was serious. She hadn't told anyone outside NBB about the CEO threatening the women's league. He could damn well fend for himself, even if he had arranged for them to see the games next weekend. If she got a chance, she'd talk to Shallcrass.

REACTIONS

Danny finally made it back to Terra Altrix and was released for two day's leave on Sunday morning. Adie had been right. The kiss had ignited the Int. The clip was endlessly recycled on talk shows, news, vlog and gossip sites, each generating more clicks for SportsLive and NBB's WWLB site. The Kiss, as it was being tagged, was the biggest bandwidth hogger that week, and had even made it into the comedy realm, with almost 1,000 spoofs and memes circulating.

She headed to Simeon's from the zoomer station. As usual, he had been tracking coverage. She barely had time to greet Bumbles before Simeon liberated a couple of beers from the fridge, sat her down and started playing the spoofs. Much to her surprise, Bumbles jumped onto the couch next to her and accepted a petting, even gracing her with a rumbling purr. Usually he ignored her for several days when she'd been away. Simeon's top choice was the anti-pornography Prime Minister and the Madam of Terra Ludus – arch-enemies in real life but represented in the throes of carnal passion. Danny's favorite was 'The Crash of the Concords' More than One Way to Play vid, with the faces of celebrities, world leaders, male and female athletes and even news anchors and sports commentators spliced into various kissing combinations. How they managed to find existing vid with the right facial expressions was incredible. Danny laughed so hard she had tears running down her cheeks at the one juxtaposing Fa'amalua's wide smile and the look of disgust on the face of the host of Adie's first seeding interview. You could almost believe the kiss had really happened. The More Than One Way to Play vid had reached 20 million hits in two days and was still growing. It ended with The Real Kiss, Adie and Danny, the tagline More than One Way to Play and a final verse from the Crash boys singing "The kiss planted the seed, so all you red-blooded men pay heed, if hot chicks are what you need, check out the Women's Basketball League."

Her 48 hours of respite meant she had time only to catch up with Vicky and Nancy for dinner, not even managing a trip to see her parents. She missed the weekly pick-up game by a day. Sunday night she slept on the couch at Simeon's, abandoned by Bumbles who chose to sleep on Simeon's bed. She felt deserted. And wondered whether she should follow Bumbles' lead. Imagining Simeon's shocked face if she wandered into his room was her last thought before falling into her first deep sleep in days.

She and Simeon talked almost nonstop. About what had happened so far, about how the public was reacting, about the next six months. On Monday, she slept late while Simeon went to work, only venturing out for a mid-afternoon run south towards Venice Beach. She avoided the beaches north of Rose Ave, wary of being seen in her own neighborhood. Her nod to disguise involved a pair of dark sunglasses and a blue beanie to hide her hair. On the beach, she ran barefoot, and even took time out to paddle in the chill of the ocean, her aching ankles reminding her that it wasn't yet summer in the northern hemisphere. When Simeon returned, they shot a few hoops on the private court tucked away in his apartment complex. It felt good to wear her own clothes, sans makeup, to sweat and even to swear a little, to not have to think about what she saying or how she was saying it. It wasn't until then that she realized how tense she had been, not until she was somewhere she could let down her guard, with someone who didn't care whether or not she was on the Int.

Simeon invited the girls over for dinner that night, explaining that Danny didn't want to go out in public. It felt like old times, just sitting around, sharing a meal. *Old times? Only a few weeks ago this was normal.* Simeon slotted into the line-up like he'd always been part of it. After dinner, he gave them time alone, claiming he had to catch up on some work.

"He's funny," were the first words out of Nancy's mouth.

"And rather swoonable actually," Vicky added. "I don't remember that part."

"Well, you usually only see the guys after pick-up games or slouched in front of the screen," she replied. "They all brush up quite well."

"I think you should let him keep Bumbles while you're away."
Nancy winked at them both. "The cat seems happy and it gives you an
excuse to keep coming back here."

"The main reason is the threats …" *Oops. I wasn't going to tell
them that.*

"Threats?" Vicky didn't miss anything. "I thought there was
only the one. But you just said threats. With an s. As in, more than
one."

Danny shrugged, trying to make out that it wasn't anything
serious.

"I got another one that sounded kind of the same, so we decided
it was safer to keep Bumbles here and for me to stay over until things
settle down. I've only been back to the apartment for clothes and to
check on the place."

"Staying over eh?" Nancy got in another wink. "And just
where have you been sleeping?"

"On the couch," she insisted a little too strongly, remembering
her imagined venture into Simeon's room. "Where else would I be?"

They both looked at her like she was mentally oh-so-slow.
Rolled their eyes.

"No," she said. "It's not like that."

"Not yet." said Vicky. "He likes you. And I think you like him
too. You wouldn't leave Bumbles with anyone you didn't trust."

"Of course I like him. He's my friend."

"Could be a lot more than a friend, I think. And I approve, by
the way. He's a bit of a dish. And smart. And he can cook. And funny.
What more could you ask?"

"Just shut up will you. We're just friends. Leave it."

And thankfully they did. Simeon returned, calling out before
he entered the room. "Anyone for coffee?" Thoughtful enough to give
them time to finish up any girl talk. They left at zero hour, leaving
Danny time for five hours sleep.

As she settled onto the couch for a second night, she couldn't
get their voices out of her head. *Swoonable. Dishy.* She'd never thought
of Simeon that way but, trying to be objective, she had to agree that he

147

was rather good-looking, all height and lean darkness. Those twinkling green eyes and an engaging smile. Smooth skin. She imagined running her fingers over his flat stomach. She'd noticed it today when he stripped off his sweaty shirt. They'd played hard. Bumping, pushing, fouling. High-fiving. Lots of touching, she suddenly realized. *Stop it. I can't think like that. Those girls are in for it.* But the thoughts persisted as she fell asleep cuddling a couch cushion.

NO REST FOR THE WICKED

And then it was back to work, Simeon dropping her at the zoomer station at seventh hour on Tuesday. Time for a quick hug (much more natural this time) before she boarded. NBB was on a mission and her wellbeing appeared to be fairly low on their list of priorities. Oh well, she had signed on for this and she was committed to the cause.

She spent five days immersed in her first taste of intensive language training. Not that she was expected to be fluent in all eight non-English languages, but NBB wanted her to be able to begin a conversation, say hello, thank you and goodbye. She started with the romance languages, Italian and French, so she asked Emilie to help her practice the French component. Then it was Spanish and Portuguese on Wednesday, German and Russian on Thursday, and Japanese and Mandarin on Friday. Saturday morning she had a short introduction to Hindi, although it was likely that most of the Regionem Indorum team and management would speak English.

She also spent far more time than she liked on makeup and dressing up for NBB standups, the pre-prepared pieces to camera highlighting the relative merits of each team in the build up to her highly publicized trips. They'd use them to promo her regular correspondent pieces while travelling. It still felt fake, unnatural, every time she had to don her TV face, and wear whatever NBB designated as the day's outfit. Emilie let her know that fashion designers worldwide were dressing her but it made little difference to Danny. She wore what she was told, when she was told, knowing all the while that her indifference drove Emilie to distraction.

"But that's a Valentalla," Emilie exclaimed preparing Danny's makeup for a studio interview.

"So? It fits. It's a bit revealing but I can live with it."

"Regarde moi. Look at me. It's a Valentalla," Emilie spoke slowly, emphasizing the point. "Everyone wants to wear him. He only takes commissions he wants. If he chooses you, you're made."

"So? I don't want to be made. I just want to be comfortable and not look like someone too old trying to dress too young."

Emilie halted her work and stepped back from Danny's face, wielding an eyeliner pencil like a baton. "You really don't realize do you? This is a really big deal. Valentalla dresses only the rich and famous. Wearing his label means you've made it. And he has incredible style. He'd never let you go out looking like mutton dressed up as lamb."

An uncontrolled 'hah' of surprise burst from Danny. She had never expected Emilie to spout one of her Dad's favorite sayings. But it was on the currency. That was one of her greatest fears. That she'd look like someone out of her time, a try-hard.

Emilie was back at work, her minted breath wafting across Danny's face as she persisted in her questioning. "Can't you feel the difference? The fabric? The cut? How you feel wearing it?'

Danny paused to think more about what she'd had to wear in the past few weeks. There were some clothes that had felt better than others, that boosted her confidence.

"Well. I like the tracksuit. The pink and black one. That feels good." Emilie just shook her head in disgust.

"D'accord?" Danny continued. "Is that right?" Emilie gave her a hum of approval. "You mean the dresses don't you?" Emilie nodded assent. "D'accord," Danny tried the word again while she thought. The days were bleeding one into the next. "The green layered thing. That felt nice and I wasn't worried that something would be showing that shouldn't be."

"Valentalla," Emilie said. "And?"

"And that yellow pleated skirt and top. They were actually quite cool – literally and metaphorically."

"Valentalla," Emilie said again. "And?"

"And I can't think of anything else. I really don't care about this stuff. I'm only doing it because they're making me." She could hear the whine in her voice.

"Nothing else you've worn is Valentalla." Emilie was triumphant. "See? He really knows how to dress someone. How to make them feel comfortable and look fantastic." Shaking her head at Danny, she continued. "You really have no idea. That skirt you wore, every knock-off outlet in the world is busy producing versions. And I can guarantee that next winter's fashions will be layers, all because he dressed you, and you looked so gorgeous."

"Gorgeous?" *Really. Who was she kidding?*

"Manifique. Truly."

"But what about Adie? She was stunning. Way more than me. Who dressed her?"

"Her usual. Jocelyn Iosefo from Terra Ludus. It was très chic but nothing out of the ordinary."

Danny was astounded. "But she looked a billion dollars. That sheath clung to every curve and she's got a gorgeous body. Who wouldn't want to look just like that?"

"You can't see yourself clearly," Emilie said. "What she wore was fine. But you were in another realm. The way that dress floated as you moved. It was as if you were walking on clouds. Astounding actually."

Danny couldn't see it, couldn't imagine it. Although Simeon had said she looked beautiful. And Dom and Con were now happily boasting that they played ball with her. Maybe there was something to it.

"So. What's next? More Valentello?"

"It's Valentalla, you ignorati," the eye-pencil firmly tapped on her head reiterating the point. "As for more. Peut être. Maybe. If you're lucky. He works for pleasure not on demand. So don't expect it, just enjoy it if they come your way. You got to keep those didn't you?"

Danny realized she had. They were both in her Mountain View hotel room and no-one had asked her to return them. She hadn't expected them to.

"You mean you don't get to keep them?"

"Of course not, mon amie. Celebrities are dressed by designers but they usually have to give the clothes back. It's a win-win. They look good and the designers get publicity. But these dresses cost hundreds of thousands sometimes, so the designers usually want them back."

Danny was surprised, and worried. How much had she been wearing? What if she'd tripped or torn something?

"But Valentalla doesn't do that. If he dresses you, whether you pay for it or not, the outfit is yours, forever. To do with what you want. To wear or not." She paused. Waggled a finger in Danny's face. "But not to sell. Not to give away. It was designed for you, and you alone."

Gaia. This is crazy. How did I get caught up in this? And how do I manage it now that I have some idea what's going on?

"Thanks for the heads up," she said. "I'll be more careful. Let me know if there's something important on the wardrobe rack, alright?"

"Oh, there will be," Emilie was adamant.

"How do you know that?" she responded. "No. Scrub that question. How will I know?" Danny couldn't help the little whine that crept back in.

Emilie was shaking her head again. "You really don't get it do you?"

"Get what?"

"You're the primary model for the League." At Danny's look of complete incomprehension, Emilie barely disguised a snigger. "No-one's told you?"

"Told me what?" Danny wasn't sure if she'd somehow entered an alternative universe.

"Told you why you're going on this trip to Terra Austalia, then to Terram Europae and Continentem Africa. Then what's next? Back here to Terra Altrix and America Meridionalis, then Asiae Nationum and Regionem Indorum?"

"That sounds about right," Danny replied, seemingly moving back onto solid ground. "And I know why I'm doing it. To spend time with the teams and interview the athletes and coaches."

"And how many appearances and interviews are you personally booked for?"

"I don't know. It looks like one or two a day in each country I think. But that's not the main reason I'm there. It's just stuff I have to do for NBB to promote the League."

This time Emilie's laughter was loud and unrestrained, as she made final tweaks to Danny's hair. "You really believe that?"

"Of course. What other reason would there be?"

Emilie unexpectedly hugged her from behind. Their expressions, side by side reflected in the mirror, couldn't have looked more different. Emilie's filled with something like motherly concern even though they were about the same age, and Danny's alight with confusion.

Emilie returned to her upright position and came around to face Danny, blocking the mirror.

"Here's the deal. And clearly no-one has explained it to you. Why do you think NBB chose these particular teams for the League?

"Well it's not because they're the best," she began hesitantly, "or Chile and Turkey would be included. I don't understand why they want Nigeria or Italy. Their national teams never even reach the world finals. They aren't even major sports markets."

"Of course they're not," came the reply. "But they all have something else in common. Any ideas?"

Danny shook her head.

"La mode, ma cherie. Fashion." While Danny digested this, Emilie continued. "Every team comes from a fashion capital. That's why there are so many Terram Europae teams. NBB has signed up a major fashion house to design for each team – the uniforms, the off-court appearances of players and coaches. And for you and the other commentators. You just watch. In each country, you'll have a different style, a different set of clothes. And you might be asked to give them back when you leave because in this case it's all about promotion. And I heard there's some deal about using basketball to promote tourism as well.

Prigging hell. Is that what I am? A clothes horse? A body to promote fashion? A travel reporter? Danny couldn't seem to formulate a response.

"Regarde moi," said Emilie. "I can see this is news to you. But you need to remember why you're here. Not what NBB wants. You're promoting women's basketball, right?" Danny nodded. "So keep your eyes on your prize and don't worry about the rest." Emilie gave her shoulder a hard squeeze. "D'accord? OK?" Making sure Danny was processing the information.

Danny nodded again. "Merci beaucoup, I think, for letting me know. So now all I have to do is focus on what I'm here for. D'accord?"

"Oui. Now get out of my chair and knock 'em dead."

TERRA AUSTRALIA

Late on Saturday, Arjun, Clive, Sally-Anne and Danny flitted to Terra Australia for four days. Their first objective was to watch the Terra Australia league final, featuring Canestri Mulier vs Sydney Ignis and do some post-match interviews. Day 2 would follow the Sydney team through an average day. NBB wanted to capture something like 'A Day in the Life Of...' Day 3 would involve more in-depth background features on all the Sydney Ignis players and support staff, including the design house that was dressing the players. Danny managed to escape that interview, leaving Sally-Anne to discuss the ins and outs of dressing a basketball team. NBB was promoting women's basketball teams as families, so everyone involved would be featured at some point in the season. Day 4 was set aside for capturing tourism-style beauty shots of the landscape and Sydney citie. Sally-Anne and Danny had this day to explore on their own, each with an icom and ipro neckband to capture more informal interactions and experiences.

"Do whatever you want," was Arjun's advice. "Just make sure it has a tourist angle of some kind. Ms Consonati trusts your judgment."

And so the rhythm of her next few months was established. In Sydney, the workday usually finished about twenty-third hour, which was fourth hour at home, much too early to make live contact. She tried to squeeze in a daily live vid to her parents, and Sim, Vicky or Nancy just before breakfast. But five minutes wasn't enough time so she resorted to me-mail and reading their messages just before falling asleep.

Each morning at sixth hour she headed out of the hotel, absorbing the feel of the citie as she jogged through quiet streets to the waterfront and past major tourist sites like the Opera House and the Royal Botanic Gardens. Although she still felt like a moving billboard, the peaceful shift from dawn to sunrise generated a calm centeredness that carried her though the non-stop 12- to 15-hour days. She was relieved to have Sally-Anne as a mentor on this first trip. And they had fun together, cementing their budding friendship as they threw themselves into making sure that women's basketball would be presented the right way. They shared breakfasts and dinners with Arjun and Clive, as the four of them developed an increasingly easy and effective working relationship. On Day 3, a glorious sunny autumn in the mid 70s Fahrenheit (she relied on her app to do the conversions from Celsius), they explored the citie together, clad in matching WWLB outfits that also subtly sported the NBB logo.

"Let's do some Vox Pop interviews as well," Sally-Anne proposed. "Ask the locals where the best places are, the best things tourists should do, and then we'll try some of their recommendations. What do you think?"

"Bonza," Danny replied, attempting a thick Australian accent, modeled on how Con sounded when he'd drunk too much. "And let's ask them what they think about the new league, and where the best Canestri courts are. Let's go for it mate!"

Together they figured out the best opening lines. "Hi, I'm Sally-Anne Lubic (or Daniela Bartoli) and I'm in Sydney to promote the new World Women's League of Basketball. Have you heard about it?" If they had and seemed to be basketball fans, they'd ask "where are best places to play pick-up ball?" If they hadn't, they'd do a bit of promotion before continuing. "I'm asking locals and visitors some questions for vids to promote the citie and the new competition. So, what are the top 5 things you'd recommend visitors should do while here?"

Then they separated, to wander the waterfront asking locals and tourists for tips and recommendations, their views on basketball, and the best things about living in Sydney.

An hour later, settled at a Circular Quay café for coffee and chocolate croissants, they compared notes and planned their day. By twenty-third hour, after a 15-hour marathon, they'd climbed the Sydney Harbour bridge, capturing magnificent vids of each other and the city from their neck bands (no loose cameras allowed), seen kangaroos, koalas and a wombat's butt at Taronga Zoo, eaten a chocolate Bilby to help save the tiny endangered bandicoot, and travelled by ferry to lunch on takeaway fish and chips on Manly beach and paddle in the ocean. In the evening, they caught sunset glinting off the shining scales of the Opera House, and ambled around the Spanish Quarter and Chinatown before heading back to the hotel to shower and dress for dinner at some upmarket restaurant in Darling Harbour that Arjun had booked them into.

"Something the sponsors are covering so dinner's on NBB," he had told them at breakfast.

"Aren't you and Clive coming as well?" Danny asked.

"No. We're spending the day in a helicopter, shooting visuals. Heading out to the Blue Mountains as well, so we'll be back late. We'll grab something on the way."

"That doesn't seem very fair," Sally-Anne chipped in. "You've been working as hard, if not harder, than we have. But we get the perk and you don't."

"That's what happens when you're a dolly," he riposted. "All the glory and none of the effort."

"Hah!" said Danny. "I think we've all been putting in long days. You agree Clive?"

Clive's usual response, a shrug of the shoulders, was all she got in reply.

"I'll take that as a yes then. Alright. What time do we need to be there? And do we need to do the dolly thing?

"Twenty-first hour – the late sitting – and, yes. Dolly up please. Dresses and shoes will be delivered to your rooms today. And make sure you record it – pix, voice, vids – and say nice things. You're on the job, not on vacation."

"A free dinner with strings," Danny sighed theatrically, as Sally-Anne quickly followed up with, "Isn't that always the way! Guess we'll just have to suffer through it. Sorry guys."

BACK TO TERRA LUDUS

The early-morning flitter raced Sally-Anne back to Terra Altrix in the same time it took Danny, Clive and Arjun to complete the three-hour standard airline flight to Terra Ludus. The next few days would more-or-less repeat the Sydney format. The first day would be with the team, capturing images of training and practice, living arrangements, diet, and how the players and coaches spent their downtime. Day 2 would be in-depth interviews with the players, coach and support staff, as well as a second interview with Kiwane Shallcrass, the only Terra Ludus referee selected for the new competition. Day 3 was the tourist day. Danny decided to take the same approach they had used in Sydney, although it would be different doing it alone. *It'll be strange to act like a tourist in a citie I know well. I guess it could be interesting to see it through different eyes, but I still want to show people my favorite places. And I've never had to try and capture Ākarana citie in one day.*

Then the guys would be here for the DELTS game. She'd have to make sure she got a decent night's sleep before they arrived.

The interviews with Canestri Mulier didn't feel like work at all. She'd already spent so much time with them that it was more like hanging out with friends. The interviews flowed well, including with the all-female crew of administrators, CEO, trainer, physio and doctor who would support the team during the season and hopefully into the quarters, semis and finals series. She didn't try to be objective. NBB hadn't specifically asked her to and she already knew her heart was with CM, not least because of her longstanding friendship with Denise.

She'd done her first local Int interview before she talked to designer Jocelyn Iosefo as part of the 'support crew' interviews on Day 2. Danny had already begun to appreciate the skill that went into making a presenter look good, noting that Jocelyn had chosen completely different fabrics and styles for Danny than she had for Adie's kissing dress. While Clive and Arjun discussed where to set up in her design studio, Jocelyn told them both to call her Joss and said she was looking forward to talking about the process. Following Arjun's thumbs up, Danny started the interview.

"I have to confess I don't know anything about fashion," was her opening line.

Joss smirked and said, "Neither do any of my sport-obsessed family and, what's more, they don't even care. I suspect you might be in the same category."

Danny's wry expression confirmed it. "But," Danny said, "I do see that you're dressing me in completely different fabrics and styles than you did for Adie Supruniak's 'kissing' dress. How do you make decisions like that?"

"Do you actually want to know?" Joss quizzed her seriously.

"Yes, actually I do. And so do our viewers. We're interviewing all the designers to find out how they make their choices for the teams and what they're trying to achieve. So how about it? Let's start specific. How did you approach dressing me, compared with Adie?"

"Well. That's a good question. Actually, I've been dressing Adie for a few years now, so I know her body, her colors and her style. So that was quite easy. She and I have talked a lot about fashion so I didn't really need to know anything except what the show was, and what Adie wanted to achieve."

Danny interrupted, unable to stop herself. "And did she say she wanted to look like sex-on-a-stick?"

Joss burst out laughing, a deep throaty gurgle that started in her belly. It was a few moments before she recovered. Arjun had turned away, his right hand clamped over his mouth to stifle the noise. Even Clive was sniggering silently as he tried to keep the camera steady.

"What?" said Danny, staring pointedly at Clive. "I just asked a question. A legitimate one I think. Adie looked amazing and that dress clung to every curve. I could never wear anything like that."

"And that's the point," Joss gasped, beginning to recover. "Each person is different, and it's a matter of figuring out what will work for them. That's my style. I usually spend a lot of time talking with them, and listening to what they say. Then I ask them to provide pix of their own clothes, the ones they feel good wearing. And I ask for vids, any kind, so I can watch them move in their clothes."

"But you didn't do any of that for me," Danny replied.

"You're right that I didn't talk to you," she said. "But I did all the other things. Once I knew I'd be dressing you for this trip, I watched all the vid. I could see which clothes you preferred, just by how you carried yourself. So I've tried to work with that. And…" Her expression seemed to be asking for feedback.

"And," said Danny carefully, wanting to be clear. "I liked what I wore last night for the studio interview. It was lightweight but still warm enough for wearing outside. The fabric wasn't too clingy and didn't bunch up when I was sitting. I don't usually wear that dark brown color but it looked alright. So, yeah, it was pretty good actually. Thanks."

"My pleasure. And I mean that. You're an interesting person to dress. Although you're as tall as most models, you have a much more normal body. And athletes are also challenging because you all have muscles, so standard sizes don't usually work well. But, to go back to your earlier question, the blue I used for Adie isn't your color. You need deeper, richer shades and I thought that dark chocolate would complement your eyes."

"Well thanks. And I look forward to seeing the next option." Danny paused, remembering what Emilie told her about designers wanting their creations returned, and now wondering if she'd spilled anything on the dress at dinner. "Do you want them back?"

"Back?"

"You know. Do you want me to give the clothes back when I leave? I heard that designers usually do."

"Not in this case. NBB is covering all the costs and it's great publicity for me, so no worries. You can keep them. Sweet as."

Danny's look of relief was obvious, prompting Joss to ask, "Why were you so worried?"

"Oh. Well. I have a tendency to be pretty hard on clothes and I've been freaking out a bit about ripping or spilling food on something really expensive. I mean, before this job, I mostly lived in sweat pants and sports clothes, with the occasional pair of dress pants and shirt for a face-to-face interview. This is a whole new ball game for me."

"Well don't worry too much," Joss consoled her. "I don't think you'll be asked to give anything back. So just wear them and enjoy it. Now, do you want to talk about the process for designing the team uniforms?"

"Sure. Can you reveal what they'll look like?"

"Not yet unfortunately, because we're still in the design phase. But I can talk about the process. It's one of the few times I've done anything for sport. And, believe me, my status has improved a lot in the 'aiga because of it."

"'Aiga? Is that like whānau or family?"

"Ioe. Yes. It's Samoan. Like I said, most of my family are mad sportspeople and I'm not. One of my extended 'aiga played for the All Blacks, although I didn't know him, and a couple of my cousins are playing professional rugby league, so they think there's something wrong with me! Getting this commission has been sweet, as long as they don't think I'm botsing it, you know, acting like I know it all."

"Great word," Danny acknowledged the slang. "I guess you'll know after this interview airs! So how do you come up with the designs? How long does it take?"

"We've been working on them since just before the announcement, so a couple of weeks. I've watched a few practices and games, live and vids, and talked to the girls and Denise about what they like. They've been sending me pix and vids. It'll take some work to find a style that works for all of them, they're such different sizes and heights and colorings. I'm finding it fascinating."

"What limits have the league put on what you can do?" Danny realized that, in her experience, you were just given uniforms and wore them, whether you liked them or not. The idea that someone was actually thinking about what would work had never crossed her mind. She loved interviews like this that took her to new ways of seeing the world.

"Not much surprisingly," Joss said. "They want different colors for each team, so that's probably going to be the most contentious. But the other designers seem to think that black is depressing, whereas here it's one of the main national sporting colors, so I think it will be some variation on black, silver or white. As for style, as long as we can fit the WWLB and team logos on the uniform, it's pretty much completely open."

"And is that an advantage or a disadvantage?"

"A bit of both. It's certainly challenging the players and the coach right now. I've had to set up a Pinterest board of sports and fashion images to trigger them to think beyond baggy shorts and tank tops. All I've learned so far is that they don't want a one-piece. You should hear them rag on the old Aussie uniforms."

"They were horrible," Danny agreed. "I can't believe the players put up with them for so long. I've always been a fan of the baggy short approach myself. Anything wrong with that?"

"Yes and no," Joss replied. "From a fashion standpoint, they're pretty boring and they don't do anything to show off the marvelous physiques of the players. So I'm trying to encourage them away from that. There are lots of choice options out there. It's just a matter of working through them."

"So how are you going to do that?"

"Two ways," Joss said, propping her icom on her design desk and opening to her Pinterest uniform pix. Clive closed in over their shoulders. "See here? There are lots of possibilities. So I've asked them to discuss and choose 2 or 3 different options. I'll make some suggestions as well. Then we'll pick three different players and make a version of each choice for each of them. We'll try a range of fabrics, although they're already pretty clear what attributes it needs..."

Danny jumped in with her next question, "And what are they?"

"Nothing surprising I don't think. Wickability, to get sweat away from the skin, but dry enough they can wipe their hands or faces on the material to get sweat off, not too tight so they don't have to worry about their body shape or size – there are some big girls in that team, and I don't just mean height-wise. And they don't want too much skin on display. It's something I've noticed in TL women. They tend to hide rather than flaunt their attributes. So I'm working with that, while trying to inject a bit more fashion and style."

"How long do you think it will take?"

"They need to be happy with the final product, so we'll take whatever time is needed. We just need to be ready for the launch in just over five months."

Arjun signaled that time was running out, so Danny began to wrap up the interview.

"Thanks for filling us in Joss. It was fascinating to find out how you go about designing a uniform from scratch. Unfortunately, that's all the time we have today, so I'd like to thank Terra Ludus designer Jocelyn Iosefo for her time. I know we're all looking forward to seeing the outcome of this very collaborative process."

THE GAME

The next day, she was at the Ākarana citie flitter port, striving for a laid-back 'hey this is pretty normal' exterior, as Mike, Dom, Con and Simeon arrived.

"Hey guys. What's up?"

"Hey girl. What's up with you? I thought you were still on Terra …." Simeon's pause extended as he processed the lower temperature and higher humidity in the air. "You are still on Terra Ludus aren't you?"

She nodded.

"And that means we are too," followed up Constantin.

"And that means basketball," they all yelled at once, startling birds into flight and drawing attention from the men unloading their bags.

She broke out in a little jig. "Oh yes it does. Sorry to break it to you but there's no fancy dinner. Instead, we've got tickets to both semi-finals!"

She found herself swept off the ground into a bear hug by Con. "You little beauty. How'd you do it?"

"Oh, no biggie. Just pitched the idea to NBB and they went for it."

"And what's the catch?" Simeon wondered aloud. "There has to be one."

"Oh, not much. They might want to interview us briefly, and one of you might get picked for the half-time shootout. And there'll probably be a camera on us some of the time. A small price to pay for courtside seats, at least for the DELTS game, don't you think?"

To Dom's "Yeah" and vigorous fist pump, she said, "Come on then. No time to waste. Game 1 starts in 15 minutes."

By the time they arrived at the stadium, and met Manu, the first quarter was underway. They were ushered to the BAI suite by the league's PR manager, who introduced herself as Candace. "We'll interview you at half-time if that's OK. We just need a few words about being fans of Deltan and men's basketball and a group photo."

"Where will it go?" queried Simeon.

"The usual," she replied. "Website, all our social media outlets. Nothing to worry about. We'll tweet to hashtag WWLB for a bit of cross-promotion. Any other questions?"

No-one said anything so Candace waved them into the compact space, explaining that food and drink were on the League, and all they needed to do was select from the icoms at their seats and it would be delivered.

"Not quite five star dining but not far off it," announced Dom, scrolling through the options. "And plush seats and a great view. Can't ask for much more than that. Hey, Mike, slide the window open so we can hear everything."

"This is amazing," Simeon whispered as he slid into a seat next to her. "You did good."

"I did, didn't I?" She couldn't wipe the grin off her face. "I was sitting in my hotel room two weeks ago realizing that the game was going on below me – right here – and I wondered if there was a chance to convince Imelda to bring you all over. So I pitched it via Arjun and she went for it. I never thought she would, or the BAI CEO either. But here we are."

"And I can't believe you didn't tell me." Simeon's statement was belied by his look of satisfaction. "How the hell did you manage that?"

"Mike," she said. "He can actually keep a secret when he really has to. And I wanted it to be a real surprise, something none of you would ever expect."

They settled in to watch the game, interrupted only by the half-time interview, filmed in the suite with the stadium crowd as a backdrop. The guys nearly tumbled over each other to talk about the experience and thank the BAI for the chance to actually see the games live. Then Candace drew Danny aside for a one-on-one. She was truly excited to be there so decided to cut the CEO some slack and let her fandom show through. They asked her the same questions – about the difference between live and Int-TV, and her thoughts on how Deltan would perform. *Testing to see if I'm a real fan.* She said whatever came to mind and finished with the agreed plug for the WWLB.

"It's fantastic to have the chance to watch my favorite team play, alongside my buddies and Terra Ludus waka ama champion Manu Paraone," she said. "The atmosphere here is amazing, as I'm sure it will be for the women's league. As you can tell, I'm a major fan of both men's and women's basketball so I hope everyone here tonight will give the World Women's League a try as well."

Interviews done, they relaxed into the second half, hoping DELTS would have the chance to play one of these teams in the finals. They joked, argued and debated the merits of various players. *Just like any other Saturday – except that it really is surround sound! And smells, and tastes and live action.*

"It's nothing like Int-TV. You've wrecked it for me," Mike half-jokingly complained. "How am I supposed to watch from home any more?"

"Oh get over it, and just enjoy it," she mocked him. "It'll never happen again in your lifetime."

"Gaia, you're right," he said. "I'll need evidence." And he extracted a miniature ipro camera from his pocket and settled it over his right ear to record the second half. "

She threaded her way over to Dom, now sitting alone.

"What's up? Aren't you enjoying it?"

"Yeah. Sure. Sorry. It's just…"

"It's just what?" She kept her voice quiet, recognizing he might not want the others to hear.

He took some time to respond. "It's just that this was my dream. To play professional ball. Here. On Terra Ludus. And being here, seeing it, smelling it, hearing it…I don't know. I'm not sure what I think, how to react."

She leaned back, absorbing the situation then turned towards him, gave him a quick shoulder bump of support. "It's not all it's cracked up to be, you know," she tried to console him. "I missed home terribly. How about this?" she suggested. "Maybe just don't think. Just be here in the moment and process it all later." She elbowed him in the side. "I mean, you have to admit it's pretty cool for all of us to be here, and for free!"

A small smile. "Yeah. I know. Just give me a minute and I'll snap out of it."

"Sure. Then get on over and enjoy it with the rest of us. May as well make the most of the free food and drink."

At the end of Game 1, Candace returned to escort them to their seats for Deltan's game, handing each of them a Delts "Road to the Finals" t-shirt to wear. They were seated in threes, one row immediately behind the other. The front group comprised Simeon, Danny and Manu in row four, with Con, Dom and Mike in row five, at center court facing the main broadcast cameras. Just about the best seats in the house and Danny appreciated the thoughtful seating choice. Now they could talk to each other, although right now, this close to the band and cheerleaders, it was so loud they could barely hear anything else. So much was going on. Advertising, dancers, music blaring, the constant buzz as people moved around the stadium stocking up on food and drinks, taking toilet breaks, stretching, you name it. *You miss all this on Int-TV coverage,* although Danny thought maybe that was a good thing. If she hadn't known that the cameras might be on them, she would have blocked both ears. It certainly hadn't been like this when she played.

The team introductions began and the stadium darkened, the only source of illumination coming from strobe lights weaving across the crowd, fan lightsticks and the dim glow from ipros recording. Then came the two-minute 3D court projection, impossible to believe it wasn't actually real as the court appeared to rise, fall, then turn itself over and inside out. Then the four huge video screens lit up with music, commentary and video highlights of each team's progress to the semi-finals and the winners' trophy, punctuated by nostalgic black and white images of basketball from the turn of the century, all accompanied by a slow, deep male voiceover designed to ensure the crowd understood the importance of the moment. Pure theatre. Like everyone around them, they stood, drawn upwards inexorably by the stadium announcer's "It's time to get on your feet. Let's hear it for your DELTANS." Danny couldn't help it – she punched her fist straight up and yelled into the combined fan roar. A spotlight followed each player onto the court as his stats and video highlights appeared on screen. Then the same for the other team. The crowd was already in a frenzy, chanting DELTS, DELTS, DELTS or SPARTA, SPARTA, only quietening down for the national anthems. Roars of support raised the decibel level again as the lights came on and both teams warmed up. Just in case they weren't excited enough, the video screens encouraged fans to "Get Loud".

In a quiet break, Danny reminded them that NBB and the host broadcaster might have cameras on them. "No picking your noses or scratching your asses," she warned. "No spilling food or yelling abuse. OK?"

"Quit taking all the fun out of it," Mike grumbled half-heartedly. "Don't worry. We'll behave. Well, we'll try anyway."

The first quarter went by in a flash. DELTS up by 2 in a see-sawing game. They were loud and unrestrained, cheering everything good. Mike struggled to hold back when the refs made bad calls but she could see he was trying hard. Every break in play was a chance to advertise. Couples encouraged to kiss sponsored by a mouthwash brand, wave your FirstBank card to win $1,000 credit, spend $100 on your Visa card to win back the price of your ticket, compete in this quarter-time competition to win a washing machine. *A washing machine? Really? What happens if you aren't from TL? Will they ship it to your home terra?* It was almost too much, the flashing video screens and stadium announcer demanding attention even during play. *Capitalism and promotion to the extreme. I hope they don't do this for our league.*

By half-time, DELTS were clinging to a 1-point lead. Only Manu seemed relaxed, crowd-gazing, soaking up the atmosphere, his broad smile a counterpoint to the frowns and tensed shoulders of Danny and the guys. "E hoa mā," he said, looking around. "Time to chill out. It's only a game."

"Only a game!" Mike nearly exploded out of his seat before realizing Manu was joking. Sheepishly he sat back down. "Yeah.

Right. It is only a game. But a really important one. They need to win Game 1 to put the pressure on Terra Sparta."

"I know bro," Manu responded. "But it isn't life and death. Cheer them on, sure, but don't give yourself a heart attack over it. Did you know you kept kicking the back of my seat?"

"Nope. Sorry 'bout that. I get a bit carried away."

"A bit," retorted Con. "That's the understatement of the decade." He and Dom smirked at Mike who gave up and wiped the frown off his face.

"OK. You win. I'm way too invested in this."

Then Candace was just in front of them, courtside, waving to attract their attention, her forefinger pointing at Dom and then to the court, as the announcer indicated that the half-time shoot out was about to happen.

"What'd you do to deserve this?" Con demanded. "It should be me. Mate, you can't shoot threes for prig."

"Now, now. Jealousy will get you nowhere. The lady chose me. Maybe she was wowed by my good looks and personality." Con blew a raspberry of disbelief as Dom continued, patting Con gently on the arm as if he was a child. "Just sit back and watch how it should be done."

Dom was the last of four competitors. His normal good spirits seemed to have returned, and he turned it on for the crowd, hyping them up, demanding their support as he walked to the designated spot outside the three-point line, repetitively raising his arms in a controlled, straight-armed movement from below shoulder height to clap above his head. Danny stood and matched his motion, then they all did, chanting "Dom, Dom, Dom, Dom". He took his first shot. Swish. Moved on to spot number 2. Swish. They yelled their support along with the crowd. Third spot. Swish. Fourth. Rimmed out – a miss. If he made the last, he'd win. No-one else had scored more than three. His fifth and final shot arced high and dropped straight through the basket. The guys fist-pumped and screamed 'yeah' as Dom walked away with the prize – a year's worth of Terra Ludus beer. In the face of the interviewer's surprise at his shooting skills, Dom admitted he'd trialed for a pro team and played regularly. "I'm a long-time DELTS fan," he said, "and being here is a dream come true. And then to win a year's supply of Whaingaroa beer. That's just icing on the cake."

"And where are you from?"

"Terra Altrix – California," he replied. "I'm here with Daniela Bartoli, helping to promote the new women's league. It's a different experience from this but it's gonna be great." Then he turned to the crowd and finished up with "Thanks for the support. And GO DELTS!" which got him a rousing cheer as he headed back to his seat.

"You sneaky deadeye..." Mike obviously couldn't think of what to add next so he just stopped midsentence. "And a year's worth of beer. Unbelievable. This day just keeps getting better. Want to store it at my place?" he ventured.

Dom just laughed. "Yeah. Right. It'd last all of a few weeks. Not a chance. It's staying with me but I'm prepared to share it when there's basketball on. OK?"

"Works for me," said Simeon.

"No objections at all," added Con.

The buzzer drew them back to the second half but just before the whistle blew, Danny turned to Dom. "Thanks for the plug," she said. "You didn't have to do that."

"Of course I did. That's the reason we're here. And, anyway, I didn't say anything I didn't believe. The new league will be good I think. And, more importantly, it'll keep you fully employed and give me and Con a few more chances to win some Saturday games!"

She launched a quick punch at his stomach, his 'oooph' a highly satisfying response as she turned back to the game. By the end, she'd nearly lost her voice. DELTS took out Game 2 of the three-match series by 5 points. Danny croaked her way through a couple of short interviews with NBB and the TL station, which also did an interview with Manu. All their responsibilities done, they headed towards the exit arm-in-arm, a sinuous line snaking their way through the crowd. Buzzing. Fizzing. Danny imagined bubbles of joy rising all around them into a cloud of happiness. This was one of those moments, one she would always remember. Unable to contain herself, she twirled out of the line and half-danced, half-skipped ahead, singing lines from DELTANS' team song, as the guys broke apart to follow her.

AFTERMATH

Settled at the hotel bar several hours after the game, she checked her messages. The first title looked innocuous enough – Saw you tonight – so she opened it. 'You don't listen very well do you?' the text began. 'You've already had two warnings. But oh no. Instead of shutting yourself down, you decide to flaunt yourself in the BAI. Your presence is an insult to the real game. This is your last warning. I know your schedule, I know your routines. You might have hidden your cat away but you're public property now. No hiding for you. So when you think you're safe, think again. I'll be waiting.'

It was a good thing she was sitting down or she would have collapsed as the blood rushed out of her head. Just like that, the happiness dissipated like spring blossoms in a brisk wind. Slowly, unwilling to draw attention, she rotated her barstool 180 degrees so she could scan the room. She silently handed her icom to Simeon, sitting beside her. The force of his fist pounding the bar rattled all their glasses. Her heart gave a huge thump and then seemed to stop working altogether. Across the room Con and Dom were so busy trying to figure out the refurbished jukebox that they didn't even notice.

"What's up?" Mike snapped. "You nearly gave me a heart attack."

"I think he did give me one," Danny gasped, finally remembering how to breathe.

"Another threat against Danny," Simeon growled. "That bastard. If I get my hands on him…" He didn't get any further before Mike interrupted.

"Threat? What threat? What are you talking about? This is a joke right?" Hesitantly, because Danny's pallor and Simeon's expression made it pretty clear something was seriously wrong.

"No joke," Simeon growled again. "This is the third time this guy's written something threatening to Danny."

"And what are you doing about it?" Mike was now standing, chest in Simeon's face. "If you knew about it and I didn't, what are YOU doing about it?"

"Everything I can," he said quietly. "But I haven't made any progress. All I know is that he – it has to be a guy – is most likely somewhere here on Terra Ludus but he's covering his tracks. We can't isolate his whereabouts."

Danny tapped his shoulder and he rotated towards her. "What do you mean covering his tracks? I thought it was safe now. I thought the threats were nothing more than piss and vinegar." *Another oldie but goodie. Gaia. I'll never get my parents out of my head.*

This time Mike forcibly spun Simeon's stool back towards him. "What threat specifically?" his voice and volume rising. "She's my friend too. I've known her a lot longer than you. Tell me."

By now Danny was on her feet and tugging Mike back onto his stool as Con and Dom returned, drawn by the noise and unusual body language.

"Tell him Sim," she said. "They probably all need to know. But not here. Let's find somewhere more comfy to sit down. I can't deal with this on a bar stool."

The late hour gave them plenty of choices so they shifted to a couple of couches in a semi-private corner. And Sim spelled it out. Three threats. The first targeting her and Bumbles, the second just Danny and this one tonight, less than an hour after the game was broadcast.

"How do you know they're linked?" demanded Mike who was now reading the contents on Danny's phone.

"Trust me. They are. The language, tone and sentence structures are similar and this one refers back to the first and the second, which pretty much nails it in my book."

"Call the Peacekeepers Danny," Dom demanded. "Call them now. Don't mess around..."

"I'll do it," said Con already heading towards the hotel reception.

"Stop Con," Danny called. "Just wait a minute. I need to think."

"No you don't," he replied. "This is simple. Threat. Evaluate. Respond."

"It's not that simple," she answered. "There's NBB and the new league to consider. The effect of making this public. The best way to deal with it."

"You're wrong Danny. It is that simple. You've been threatened. We take action."

"Oh stop being all Rambo about it," she teased weakly. "Let me contact NBB and discuss how they want to deal with it. I'll report it or they will, but hopefully not in a way that escalates it. He (or she) hasn't done anything yet. This could be another empty threat, just meant to scare me. Which it's done I admit." Accompanied by an involuntary shiver, she finished with, "And I'm not looking forward to going to my hotel room."

"OK. OK. You can deal with it but I want to know you've reported it before any of us leave here. And you're not sleeping alone. I'm coming with you to make sure you're safe."

Even as scared as she was, Danny couldn't resist the opportunity, since he'd left himself so wide open. She laid on the sarcasm thick and heavy. "Oh Constantin. Thank you. I never knew you cared. But I'd always hoped our first time together would be a bit more romantic. You know, flowers and candles, that kind of thing."

Muffled snorts from Mike and Dom, incomprehension from Con and something she couldn't quite read from Simeon. Then Mike and Dom were laughing unrestrainedly, joined by a red-faced Con who'd finally figured it out.

"That's not what I meant. And you know it. I just meant…"

"We know what you meant," inserted Simeon seriously. "And you're right. Danny shouldn't be alone tonight. I have Monday off so I can afford a night without sleep. You three can't and we all have to be up early for the flitter home. So, if it's alright with Danny, I'll stay with her tonight, after she's talked with NBB and this threat's been reported." At Danny's tiny nod, he stood up. "So let's put what was, until just now, a fantastic evening to bed."

Mike rolled his eyes at Simeon but rose and gave Danny a hug, saying "You're right. And thanks Danny. This is quite possibly the best day of my life." Turning to Dom and Con, "C'mon you two. Let's hit the sack. We've got a wake up call for seventh hour. Sim, I'll bring your stuff to Danny's room – 1218 right? Just down the hallway."

"I'm scared," she admitted, tucked between the sheets of the super-king bed. "The first one freaked me out when I first read it, but the second time I didn't really believe they were linked. And when nothing happened, I stopped thinking about it." She rolled onto her side, facing away from him as he sat propped against the bedhead on top of the covers, still in his shirt and pants. He only just heard her whisper, "But this really scares me. I don't know what to do."

"How about this?" he said, sliding down and curling himself around her back, resting his arm across her body over the bedclothes. "You're safe now and I'll get my best people on it tomorrow. They'll re-run Psychia and some other new programs we're testing to confirm if it's just some strange coincidence or the same person. And I'll discuss with NBB what we find …"

Exhaustion overtook her quickly as his warmth seeped into her. She was asleep before Simeon finished the sentence, so he stayed where he was and let her quiet breathing still his anger.

She woke to the sound of Simeon's voice, followed by his hand on her shoulder. The shades were only slightly raised, letting in a hint of dawn. "Hey," she said.

"Hey. Sorry to wake you but we've got to go in 30 minutes. I let you sleep as long as I could."

"Thanks," she mumbled still snuggled under the covers but noting that he was still wearing last night's clothes. "Did you get any sleep?"

"Some," he said. "Pulled the bedcover over me and dozed off for a while."

"Some guardian you are," she joked. "Good thing the boogeyman didn't try to attack while you were snoring."

"I don't snore," he retorted but there was no smile in response to the first part of her joke. Both of them turned towards the door at the sound of a quiet knock. Simeon rose, collected his bag and looked through peep-hole before opening the door. "I'll grab a coffee and make sure everyone's ready," he said. "Set the deadbolt once I leave. We'll meet you in the lobby in 20." With a wave and a smile, the door shut behind him, followed immediately by his rat-a-tat-tat farewell knock.

Aware she was only wearing a t-shirt and briefs, and wondering if he knew this, she did as told, ensuring that all the locks were engaged, before she hit the shower.

They parted ways in Mountain View. She headed to her hotel, deciding to skip her planned run for today. She didn't want to be outside alone even though she needed the exercise.

TRAVELLING

Over the next four months, she developed a steady running routine. Sim had confirmed to NBB that the threats were generated in Terra Ludus so she should be cautious when there but should have no problems elsewhere. Although Imelda expressed the view that Danny would be safe, even on Terra Ludus, she agreed to Simeon's suggestion that NBB disguise her travel schedule and not reveal when she would be on Terra Ludus, although it would be obvious if she did anything live-to-Int.

No matter which citie Danny found herself in, she emerged from her hotel room sometime between fifth and sixth hour, aiming to run into sunrise. There was always a hotel concierge with enough English to direct her along a safe and sometimes scenic route. She ran alone, seeking peace on the almost-empty streets and paths, wherever possible seeking higher ground, the wider view. In urbanities where her app showed pollution levels were too high to be outdoors, she used the gym or indoor swimming pool. On her tourist day, she spent as much time as possible outdoors, absorbing the feel of the place and its people. It would be useful knowledge once the season started, no matter what role she ended up in.

In Paris, they were based in the 15th arrondissement, about five blocks from the Seine. She ran daily along the river, encountering famous monuments at every turn – the Louvre, Notre Dame, the Eiffel Tower, the bridge of lovers' locks. She saw them all without crowds, quiet and peaceful in the lightening dawn. She vlogged it all, including her frequent attempts to dodge early morning dog owners and their pets' morning ablutions, thinking it would give viewers a different perspective from the standard day-time tourist experience of long queues in the hot Paris summer sun. On her official tourism day, needing some time by herself but with little faith in her capacity to effectively express herself in French, she avoided her usual local interviews and explored randomly, discovering tempting patisserie tucked into eight-storey apartment blocks adorned with intricate ironwork, ancient cemeteries, parks full of sculptures, and frequent unexpected peeks of the Eiffel tower. The buildings and streets were redolent with age and history, especially compared with Terra Altrix and Terra Ludus. She spent several hours in Parc André Citroën on near the bank of the Seine, a quiet and peaceful 35 acres on the site of a former Citroën car manufacturing plant. With mature hedging, white gravel paths, secluded seating areas, playful fountains, and free public toilets, she chose it as the place to savor a lunch comprised solely of fresh strawberries.

In Illicium, she struck up an unexpected friendship with the Shanghai-based coach, Linxiu Liu.

"Nín hǎo," Danny began with the respectful form of hello. "Zǎo. My name is Daniela Bartoli."

"Good morning Daniela," the coach replied in almost accentless English. "Call me Lynn. My Chinese name sounds like Lynn-Shoe in English so Lynn is close enough for me."

"Xièxiè. Thank you," Danny repeated in English, having learned that she was completely deaf to Chinese tones and not wanting to offend. "And please call me Danny. I only use Daniela in formal situations."

For the tourist day, Linxiu arranged an overnight visit to her home city, Chengdu, the provincial capital of Sichuan province. Arjun and Clive agreed, because the giant pandas of Chengdu would make great vid. Linxiu, it seemed, had other plans. She wanted Danny to fully understand the team culture she had created for players from all over Illicium. On Day 2, the interview day, she explained her philosophy.

"I come from Chengdu, the slow city of Sichuan province," she said. "And that's one reason I am in Shanghai. According to Sichuan lore, I am too young to appreciate Chengdu life. In Chinese, it is written like this, as she rapidly sketched the characters with a fingernail on her icom. 少不入蜀，老不出川. It means you had better not come to live in Sichuan during your adolescent time. Because Sichuan is rich and leisurely, you will live at ease and forget your dreams. But please stay in Sichuan in your declining years, because you can live comfortably in your retirement. In Chengdu we say something like 'Live slowly, get your ears cleaned, and play mahjong'. It highlights the value of balancing work and relaxation, and sharing time with friends and family."

"Get your ears cleaned?"

"Yes. We translate the Chinese word to 'ear leisure'. You will see when we arrive. And I invite you to experience it."

Danny was pretty sure this wouldn't be on her high priority experience list. But it was certainly unique so maybe she should try it. She'd already built a committed audience for her tourism vlogs, their comments suggesting that they liked her relaxed approach, emphasis on local knowledge, and ability to find lesser-known experiences and places.

"That is why I encourage the girls to play Sichuan mahjong in their downtime," Linxiu continued.

"But they didn't seem very relaxed in how they play," Danny commented. "It looked pretty competitive to me."

"That is because they are top athletes. I do not think they can do anything without competing. But mahjong means they play together, and the games can be played quickly so they like that."

After a special trip to see the giant pandas, Linxiu received permission to take Danny, Clive, Arjun and the players into Chengdu's Jinli, a restored example of Chengdu's ancient leisure life. This was the realm of the ear-cleaners.

"Some of the girls will take this leisure," Linxiu explained, "but, as our guest, we want you to be the first." As Arjun whispered in her ear, "you have to do this," Danny noted Clive's frown as he assessed how to compensate for the relative darkness. The streets were lit only by Chinese paper lanterns that added to the relaxed ambience but provided little illumination. She took a seat, out in the open air, as people walked by or stopped to watch.

As the process began, she realized she hadn't asked what kind of training was required to be an ear-cleaner, or whether they had to be certified. She had swallowed the ear-leisure philosophy without question, and now it was too late to withdraw. *What were you thinking?* her mental critic muttered. *Don't you realize your ears are precious? You've just turned them over to someone you don't know from a bar of soap. And he's dripping (tickling?) things into your ears. And he has those long sticks. What if he punctures an eardrum?* On and on went the inner voice, as the elaborate process continued. She tried to force herself to relax, reminding herself that people did this every day in Chengdu.

"How was it?" asked her host when the cleansing was complete.

"Spooky," was all Danny could muster. "It took a lot longer than I imagined it would."

"But how do your ears feel now?"

Danny shifted her focus from fear to assessment. "Good, actually," she said. "They feel clean."

"Now do you see what I mean by ear leisure?"

"Not exactly, I'm sorry. I think I was too nervous to actually enjoy it."

"Do not worry then. Just watch the girls. They will show you why it is such a nice form of leisure."

The several players who took the opportunity had clearly done this before. Each sat still but relaxed, showing no signs of tension. While they were enjoying the process, Clive beckoned her over. "Check this out," he said. "Great vid. You look like a terrified rabbit." And she did, all wide eyes and frozen horror. "Can't wait to post this," he said. "Your fans will love it."

"How do you know I've got fans?"

"I follow your vlog," he responded. "It's surprisingly good. You've got a decent eye for an amateur videographer, and you don't take it too seriously."

"Stalker," she retorted. "If you post that, I'll block you!"

"No need for that," he said. "How about I dropbox it so you can put it into this week's vlog. Just give me a credit OK?"

"Alright," she agreed, relenting. "You've got it. I'm sure by the time I post I'll be over the shock and maybe onto remembering it as something new and exciting."

"Be honest," was his advice. "Anyone seeing that vid will know the truth. And they'll enjoy it, and probably decide not to try it for themselves. I certainly won't be."

They finished the night meandering through Jinli's streets, gawking at the food options – fried silkworms and spun sugar animals among them. They encountered a tree covered in the Chinese equivalent of the Paris lovers locks, made of silk and other material, on their way to a traditional Sichuan face-changing performance. No matter now closely she observed, she could not anticipate a single one of the many mask changes. This was another vid that was definitely going online, along with the food pix. On their way to the airport, where she observed that the slow life (or Western road rules) did not seem to apply to driving, their last stop was to admire the public statue of Chairman Mao, founder of modern China, towering nearly 100 feet above a city square.

Keeping Emilie's advice in mind, Danny tried to keep her focus on the basketball. But she couldn't help noticing that in each terra, she received new outfits. There was something different for every local interview or public event. Somewhat to her surprise, Jocelyn was correct that no-one asked her to return them. *I'll have to build another wardrobe if this carries on. My apartment's too small.* She continued the interviews with designers, discovering a myriad of different design philosophies, although none gave anything away about the actual uniform the team would be wearing. Clearly her interviews were designed to build suspense and interest in the final outcomes.

She felt the distance growing between herself and this public persona – Daniela Bartoli, the face of the World Women's League of Basketball. But there wasn't much she could do. In a small act of resistance, she sneaked out somewhere in Terram Europae and found a store that stocked incredibly soft and outrageously costly sweatpants and sweatshirts. Even though she only wore them in her hotel rooms or on days off, at least they were hers. *Thank Gaia for Santos. At least he created some space in the contract for me to be me when I'm off camera, even if that's not very often.*

She rarely made it home to Santa Monica, but managed a week's leave with her parents during the major apple-picking season.

Her parents drove her to Simeon's to see Bumbles, who barely acknowledged her presence before heading out a newly-installed cat door to the secure apartment complex garden.

"Don't worry," Simeon said. "Pretty much everyone in the complex likes him. He's the only cat here and he's always out in the garden making friends. And don't worry about me keeping him for extra time. He's not too bad for a cat. In fact, he's quite good company."

She nodded in agreement but could not shake the fear that Bumbles might no longer be her cat. Would he want to move back in with her once all this pre-launch travel was over? Oh well, she couldn't worry about that now. She'd just have to park her worries until her crazy schedule settled down.

On her parent's farm, picking apples 10 hours a day, she relished the sore muscles and physical exhaustion. She slept dreamlessly. Even out of practice, she was still one of the their top pickers. And when her parents insisted on paying her, as they always had, she transferred part of her earnings to Simeon, under the heading 'Bumbles care'.

Then it was back to work as the six-week pre-season competition got underway. She and Sally-Anne travelled extensively, as each team played home-and-away matches in four pools to build local support before all the teams shifted to Terra Ludus for the season proper. Much to her delight, Danny picked up the four-team pool of Shanghai, Tokyo, Sydney and Ākarana, and the three-team pool of Los Angeles, New York and Sao Paolo. Only in Brazil would she need a full-time interpreter. Sally-Anne was based primarily in Europe, focused on the London, Paris, Barcelona and Rome pool, and the final grouping of Berlin, St Petersburg and Abuja.

On the final flight back to Mountain View, she realized that Imelda might have been right that play-by-play wasn't the best place for her. She had a lot of studio and interviewing experience now and actually enjoyed talking to the players and coaches. Thanks to spending an extended period with all the teams, she probably knew more than anyone else about each team, and she'd built some decent relationships. Well, she'd have a chance to try out several possibilities during next week's 10–10 competition to launch the season. The WWLB took its lead from other successful short-form games like

20–20 Gryllus, Harpastan Sevens and Septum Pila Fast Five. The weekend-long tournament on Terra Ludus would involve all 14 teams, playing two 10-minute halves, competing for three different trophies. But first she and all the teams had to survive the official launch of the league.

DOWN THE RUNWAY

"Welcome everyone to the launch of the World Women's League of Basketball and its inaugural 10–10 tournament." A deep male voice boomed into the darkened stadium. Strobe lights slowly swept across the space, packed with celebrities, politicians, fashionistas and media, coming to a stop illuminating a raised platform that extended most of the length of the basketball court. Waiting in the 'home' locker room, watching images of the live coverage, Danny was plunged back into her experience of the DELTS game. *And why shouldn't I be? We're in the same space, with the same stadium announcer, same strobe lights.*

"How spooky is this?" she whispered to Denise. "We're about to make history, on a basketball court, in high heels."

"True that," Denise replied. "And the only history I want to make involves managing to stay upright. I'm not sure I signed up for this."

"Oh yes you did," Danny giggled. "When you said we're happy to do whatever you need, NBB took that literally!"

"But at least you've been in this situation before," Denise said. "When you and Adie did that kissing thing. Girl, you two really had it going on!" Then, drawing on her Southern Terra Altrix origins, she deliberately drawled, "This be a first for me, honey." Placing one hand on Danny's shoulder for balance, Denise extended a long leg to reveal a calf-length black culotte, paired with a bright pink, open-toed stiletto, and matching pink toenail polish that set off her glowing dark skin. "Seeing how you done pulled it off is the only reason I agreed to this, although the body polish, pedicure and manicure was an unexpected bonus. I figure if they done made you look good, they gonna have no problem with me!"

"Well, honey, it sure done worked," Danny drawled back. "But seriously, you look great. It's the best coach's uniform I've ever seen, excluding the shoes of course. Gaia, can you imagine trying to coach wearing those?"

"Not a chance. But these culottes do the trick. Long enough that I'm not worried about flashing something no-one wants to see and with enough stretch that I can move easily. I tried out a few options and these were by far the best."

"How did you find it working with Jocelyn Iosefo?"

"Real great. We hit it off real well and the girls loved her. One of her extended family played rugby for TL, so she's been around high-level sport and the public spotlight her whole life. She joked that her family don't know what to make of her 'unnatural' interest in fashion! So we figured she would give us something we could work with. And that's what happened. The girls love their skorts so much they've nicknamed themselves the Fluid Wahine."

"Fluid?"

"Yeah. Because they're so comfortable that they don't even know they're wearing them. Apparently the material makes them feel like they're flowing on the court. Don't ask me what that means. But they're certainly a step up from those tacky onesies that Terra Australia used to wear. Remember those? They were so skin-tight they had to wear tennis wristbands to wipe off the sweat, and they were always having to pull the material out of their butts. A real pain in the ass, eh?" Denise's hoot of laughter rang through the hot and crowded backstage area, to be followed almost immediately by an annoyed "shush" from the mistress of ceremonies.

Danny's response was pitched at the appropriate decibel level.

"Right. Times have certainly changed. And look at me, all dolled up like a princess just to launch a new sport. Couldn't play or coach in this. Ah well. I guess we better just get out there and enjoy it."

"True that again. It a-looks like time to go. Good luck out there."

Danny was first on the runway, dressed again in Valentalla to Emilie's delight. She had enjoyed introducing Emilie to Denise and some of the coaches, like Linxiu, who spoke good English. Emilie did makeup for Danny, Adie who was announcing courtside (or should that be runwayside?), and the French team who seemed relieved to be able to communicate in their own language.

She rather liked the dress, an off-the-shoulder ivory silk that draped across the front and fell in soft folds to just above her ankles, drawing attention to the strappy high heels. Thank Gaia she had run this morning, relishing the now familiar route to the top of Maungatui for sunrise. After a few hours in these shoes, who knows whether she'd even be able to walk tomorrow.

And then she was on the runway, cautiously negotiating her way to end of the platform, striking a few poses and giving the crowd a wave while trying desperately not to laugh or fall over. Denise, as coach of TL's team, Canestri Mulier, was on her way down the runway as Danny began her return. Danny winked and they gave each other their old low-five, high-five combo as they passed each other, drawing a spontaneous burst of applause.

As each terra modeled its uniform, it became obvious that NBB had given the designers completely free reign. This would not be a league where the only difference was the color of the uniform. Each team modeled some variation on skirts, skorts, shorts, leggings or knickers. Top styles included tanks, crop tops, halters and t-shirts in all manner of fabrics. Some looked like you could wear them out socially, others were clearly designed for sport. Terra Ludus showed very little skin in their mid-thigh skorts and relaxed, short-sleeved crew-necks with a nifty crossover back cut-out. The Australians looked relaxed in fitted shorts and tank tops, as did the Mumbai players in their long sleeves and loose-fitting knee-length shorts. Not surprisingly, Sao Paolo owned the catwalk in tight knickers and cropped halters.

Then it was onto the gala dinner, at tables set on the stadium floor, covered in fine linen, candles and a seemingly unlimited supply of fresh seasonal delicacies and excellent champagne. After dinner, Danny's role was to circulate, talking with sponsors and building enthusiasm for tomorrow's competition and the league overall. She drank only a few sips of champagne but plenty of water. She needed to be up early for a quick run, followed by preparation for the tenth hour start. Imelda had acceded to her desire to try play-by-play, giving her the opening game, Canestri Mulier v Los Angeles, since she knew both teams well. Then the rest of her day would be a mix of in-studio hosting and post-match coach interviews for use during Day 2.

As planned, she began the day with a quick run up Maungatui, filling her lungs with fresh air and reveling in the clear morning light. Then she scanned the online news over breakfast in her room. The TL coverage led with the headline 'Hot Babes with Hot Balls – TL hosts first basketball 10–10' alongside a small montage of glammed-up players from the dinner. Following the link, she encountered a large photo of Denise posing in her burnt orange evening dress, make up and dangling earrings, spinning a basketball on her forefinger. Viewed on the hotel room's big screen, Denise and the TL players parading down the runway looked almost human-sized. *Hot balls? Gaia! Why can't they just present it as sport?* But Danny had to admit the image was both bizarre and arresting. Denise was the local angle, discussing the 10–10 format, Canestri Mulier's likely chances, and the new league. There was also a half-page interview with Kiwane Shallcrass, the only Terra Ludan referee at the event. The article rated the experience of the referees from across the globe, making the case that Shallcrass had the experience to be selected to run the final. All the other teams appeared in their home media, as well as the league and NBB sites, with images and vid of the team and/or coach in their new uniforms or evening dresses. If there was a referee from their terra, she or he was also part of the coverage. *Well done Imelda. You've really got this thing covered.*

The tournament ended with higher ratings than expected so NBB was happy. As Danny had hoped, Imelda confirmed she would take on the studio host role when the league started next week. This meant full-time work – with games on Sundays, Mondays and Tuesdays in Terra Ludus, so the live broadcast could go out on the Saturdays, Sundays and Mondays preferred by the larger Northern hemisphere markets. And then there were the twice-weekly preview and review shows. She'd have to think about moving to TL for half the year. And that left the question of Bumbles. Would he be able to move with her? The quarantine rules for TL were sure to be much stricter than Terra Altrix, since so much tourism and income depended on tight biosecurity.

Danny was exhausted, having snatched less than 10 hours sleep in two days, but by tomorrow tonight she'd be back home for a week's leave, during which she intended to sit around in comfy clothes and do very little. Visit Mom and Dad for a couple of days, catch up with Nancy and Vic, and enjoy a few runs along the beach. A pity it was too cold for swimming. She'd shoot hoops and watch the games with the guys. Perhaps she'd head home to the apartment. Surely it was safe to do that now.

Tomorrow she would have a whole day to herself, finally enough time to head down to the marae. *The Aunties will never forgive me if I don't make it down this time.* And she needed the grounding. Her mind was still spinning, a swirling mess of fragments of languages, accents, clothes and statistics. Before dropping into a much-needed full night's sleep, she booked a driver for tenth hour and sent a quick vid letting them know she was coming.

She ran early as usual, her favorite five kilometers through the bush up to Maungatui's volcanic cone, aiming to reach the summit in time for the sixth hour sunrise while avoiding public attention. The paths weren't lit but there was enough ambient light and by now she knew her way. If she couldn't be at home, she might as well make the most of another perfect dawn. Halfway up, she was admiring the peeks of the harbor through the trees when she realized the bush was unusually quiet. Each footfall on the dirt path was audible. Usually by now, she was surrounded by the unique clicks and bell-like chimes of TL's glorious songbirds, the tui.

She felt a skittering across the skin at the back of her neck, followed by a spurt of almost scalding bile as her body was the first to recognize that something wasn't right. She began to jog faster, not quite a sprint but somewhere close to uncomfortable, seeking the corner where she might sight other morning joggers. Then a loud crack and a sudden burning in her shoulder. And another crack, accompanied by the disorienting sensation that the ground was falling up towards her. Then nothing.

CHAPTER 27

CHANGE

The first police statement was given while surgeons were operating on Danny. The chief of police announced that two people had been shot, one killed and the other in a serious condition in the main Terra Ludus hospital. No names were provided, nor would they be until the families had been notified.

Despite the police silence, it didn't take long for rumors to solidify into facts. Terra Ludus media outlets began reporting that Kiwane Shallcrass, who had spoken on behalf of the women's league and refereed the inaugural 10–10 final, had been killed by a single gunshot outside his home only an hour after Daniela Bartoli, the face of the new women's basketball league, was found unconscious and bleeding on the slopes of Maungatui.

NBB flew Danny's parents to Terra Ludus where she was treated in the private wing of the state-of-the-art hospital, by a Terra Ludus neuro-surgeon with years of experience. Not that the hospital was really designed for this kind of situation; its main focus was treating athletic injury. But the staff was experienced at dealing with the media and protecting athletes' privacy. So inside the hospital there were no cameras, no media except those officially sanctioned by NBB, and no leaks of information to a clamoring press.

Outside was a different matter. The lawn resembled a tailgate party, with TV vans and independent vid operators all vying for news of any kind. Anyone entering or leaving the hospital was fair game. The world knew that she had been shot twice, once in the shoulder and once in the head by a high-powered rifle, but that was all. The joggers who found her, alerted by a noise so unusual that one described it as sounding like a heavy book dropped on a wooden floor, were already mini celebrities, as was the hospital CEO who daily reported that

193

she was stable but still in an induced coma and that doctors had no clear idea when or if she would recover. "Brain injury is notoriously difficult to predict," he said on Day 2 (with variants on the same theme each time he was asked). "But we're hopeful. Although she's still on a ventilator, we believe she's capable of breathing on her own. She's fit and strong and the bullets have been removed. The head wound wasn't deep, and bullet doesn't appear to have done any irreparable damage but we need some time for the swelling to subside. Her family are with her."

When it became apparent the doctors would keep her sedated for at least a week, the media scrum shifted to the police station. On Day 3, the police revealed some details, explaining that the bullets appeared to be from a .22 rifle, the most common gun on Terra Ludus, most often used for hunting. The police spokeswoman attributed Danny's survival to the first shot hitting her in the shoulder. "It appears that her reaction to the initial impact of the bullet turned her body sufficiently that the second bullet grazed the side of her head with minimal penetration rather than passing directly through her brain," she announced. "Kiwane Shallcrass was not so lucky. He was shot at closer range, directly through the heart, and he died at the scene. Our thoughts are with the families," she continued, "and we have a police team dedicated to finding the offender. This is the first murder on Terra Ludus in five years. We are committed to resolving this crime." She refused to take questions.

After a week, the police released more details, including the likely shoe type worn by the shooter. The spokeswoman explained that footprints at the scene suggested size 8 boots, quite possibly Italian-made, of which just over 600 had been imported into Aotearoa in that size. She provided an image of the boot style and asked the public to call in if they had a pair or knew someone who did. She also explained that the significant tread wear at the heel and ball of the foot areas suggested the person who wore them had pronounced overpronation.

The shootings were the cause célèbre of the year. The first murder and attempted murder on Terra Ludus in years, and of two Int-world celebrities. Basketball escaped the confines of the sports pages into cross-platform coverage: news, politics, gossip and talk-back

Int, as well as its now regular appearance on the fashion and travel pages. The funeral and eulogies for Shallcrass received blanket coverage. Despite the family's request for privacy and time to grieve, peacekeepers were required to safely escort them anywhere in public. Reporters climbed trees and bribed neighbors for access to sightlines of the Shallcrass home. Someone even placed a bug on the outside walls of their house in search of an exclusive.

Danny was protected from the intense media scrutiny because she was in hospital. And because the advanced security systems on her Int-mail and other electronic devices held. Simeon knew they would. He'd installed them all himself. Something he did for his friends and anyone with whom he had regular electronic interactions. Mike and the guys and, since the last threat, Danny's close friends and family had security screens they weren't even aware of. Simeon was careful. Precise. He knew what he was doing. So despite the media's legal and illegal efforts, they couldn't find any hidden dirt on Danny. And they tried. Hard and often. He tracked the attempts, and backtracked some to their sources. NBB was one of them. Probably making sure there wouldn't be any unexpected surprises. But even they couldn't get through the myriad of complex firewalls.

Meanwhile, the publicity did wonders for public interest in the women's league. Sponsors and advertisers came flocking, and NBB raked in hundreds of thousands of new subscribers who signed up in protest at the shooter's actions and in support of Danny or Kiwane.

Ten days later, the police announced that tips from the public had led to the arrest of 38-year-old businessman and Terra Ludan resident, Hillman Dale. In the police photographs, he appeared fit but stocky, average height and well dressed. He had neatly cut, short dark hair, blue eyes, lightly tanned skin and straight white teeth. His hands appeared clean with clipped nails. There was a sweetness to his smile. Not at all what the public was expecting. It was only when he spoke that the edginess revealed itself. He didn't help his cause when a local journalist asked what he thought about the new women's competition being televised. His lawyer, ineffectually shoving his way through the media scrum towards his client who was being escorted by peacekeepers towards the courthouse for his first appearance, was unable to stop him from speaking. The peacekeepers appeared happy to stand aside as the media crowded around.

"I believe you people," Dale sneered at the journalists, "would refer to it as a 'load of crap'. It's an insult to the beautiful game of basketball. It's a man's game. It's where men learn to be men. That's the start and end of it. It's bad enough that the game allows females to play" – the insufferable sarcasm flooding his pronunciation of 'females' did much to unite the world's women – "but why NBB would pay attention to it is beyond me. I pay my Terra Ludus rates and my NBB subscription to watch real sport. I don't pay it to have inferior athleticism inflicted on me."

And he didn't help himself any more when he answered the journalist's question about how he felt about the woman reporter being shot. "I don't know her," he said, "but in my view it's not surprising what happened. It's her fault and, as far as I can see, she's responsible for what happened to her. She stirred up a hornet's nest. She's paying the price. And that man" – again the disgust flooded his voice – "he asked for it, talking about …" What he was about to say was cut short as his lawyer finally reached him, glared at the peacekeepers and hustled him away from the media scrum with a "no further comment."

The trial, which began as the inaugural women's league entered its sixth week, was mercifully brief. The evidence was overwhelming. Police had quickly found the ejected .22 shell from the bullet that penetrated Danny's shoulder, some 5 feet from the shooter's position, where it had rolled downhill into thick grass. An immediate canvass of the neighborhood surrounding Maungatui had produced a sighting, remembered because the 78-year-old witness wondered why a man in a long dark coat and cap had been up the mountain so early. Most of those who passed her window each morning were dressed in exercise gear. She was able to give police the license plate numbers of three cars, parked nearby, that she had never seen before. Within days, they had tracked him to his home in the rurality just outside Ākarana citie. Key evidence was found under a pile of pine and manuka firewood in the back yard after an extensive search of his property. Wrapped in a black gabardine coat still carrying fragments of totara bark that matched the trees in the area from which the shot was fired, police found a .22 rifle carrying traces of the shooter's DNA, and a pair of boots matching the footwear prints left in the soft mud at the scene. His ex-wife confirmed that he owned a .22 with a telescopic sight. And several workmates confirmed that he was commonly seen wearing boots of that style to work. Finally, in height and body shape, he matched a general description of a man noticed loitering near the Shallcrass home some days before Shallcrass was shot, even though he was not visible on any of the regular drone surveillance images. Circumstantial evidence linked the source of threatening emails sent to Danny and Kiwane Shallcrass to three different internet cafes, all within 100 kilometers of Ākarana citie, although no-one remembered Dale in particular.

Even when Dale's lawyers began leaking details of his early life, including the loss of both parents in a rare electrix car crash, followed by physical and emotional abuse by a series of foster families, the tide did not turn in his favor. He had overcome an horrific childhood, the lawyers argued, to become a respected businessman, only to be undone by his wife unexpectedly walking out six months earlier.

An enterprising journalist tracked down his wife, who refused to talk, but her friends were not as reticent. They described a woman worn away almost to the point of invisibility by a relentless drip, drip, drip of criticism and confidence-sapping put-downs. Against his wishes, she had taken a low-paid, part-time job in a bank – "all you're capable of," he had apparently sneered – learning the rules, calculating how to leave with half their assets. Morning tea chats with loan officers built her knowledge. The day after he turned his savage sarcasm on their four-year-old daughter was the day she left, scrupulously fair, taking half and only half of their money and possessions. The moving van had been on standby, her papers ready, the transfer to another branch in different citie already organized. When he returned home all trace of them was gone; only a Dear John letter for explanation.

The lawyers contended that, in the face of her departure, his fragile sense of self had crumbled under what he saw as an attack on his one remaining place of solace, the basketball court. They wheeled out a former coach – a steely military don't-talk-back-to-me-son type who emanated power and competence. The coach spoke about the frightened, hesitant 10-year-old he had taken under his wing and turned into a confident, assertive forward who aspired to be a professional athlete until his failure to grow put paid to that dream. In the interview, he said, "Through basketball, he learned how to be a man. And that's what I taught them all, all those broken boys. That basketball was a place to be a man, to show what you're made of." Then, with emphasis, he stated, "But I never taught them to hate women or to put down women's basketball. We never even discussed it."

GOING HOME

When it became clear that the hospital could do nothing more for Danny, NBB flew her home to Terra Altrix. Hoping the quiet of the post-Christmas break would provide some relief from media attention, they were careful not to announce the date of departure or provide Danny's address. But, drawing on the infinite resource that was the Int and social media, enterprising journalists found the information almost immediately. Realizing there was no chance of a quiet transfer, since the media was already creating disruption in Danny's Santa Monica neighborhood, NBB made the most of it. Complete with purpose-built platform, NBB held a press conference on the lawn in front of the Terra Ludus hospital. Danny's neuro-surgeon spoke first, reiterating that all the signs were good. He explained that Danny had been removed from the ventilator, was breathing on her own, and that scans indicated brain activity although she remained in a coma. Broadcast on a large screen from Terra Altrix, Simeon spoke on behalf of the family, describing how Danny would be surrounded by her parents and close friends, and requesting privacy so that she could heal. Then Manu stepped up to the microphone. Having seen the insatiable media need for information, his whānau had asked him not to share his full genealogy, as he normally would, in the hope of maintaining some privacy for their people. "Tēnā koutou e hoa ma," he began. "Ngā mihi mahana ki a koutou. Ko Manu Paraone toku ingoa. No Aotearoa ahau. Hello everyone, friends," he said. "Warm greetings to you all. My name is Manu Paraone and I hail from here, Aotearoa, a place that many of you know as Terra Ludus. I am here to let you know that my iwi, or tribe, stands beside Daniela and her family. We met her 14 years ago when she joined Canestri Mulier, a team for which my sister was then playing. Because of this connection, we welcomed the team every year onto our marae or gathering place. For some of the players, Danny among them, our marae became their home away from home. And for a rare few, of whom Danny is the only one in the last few decades, we informally adopted her as part of our iwi. So when she was hurt, so were we. We stand beside her parents, Valerie and Elario, and will continue to tautoko and support them through this difficult time. NBB has kindly agreed to cover the cost of flights so that someone from our whānau can be with them at all times, starting with my mother. As for me," he concluded, "Danny is like a sister to me and perhaps to many of you listening. We welcome your thoughts and prayers and know that you, like all of us, are hoping for the very best outcome. If you truly want to help, buy a subscription to the thing she cared about most, the World Women's League of Basketball. Showing your support in this way is the best thing you can do for her. No reira, tēnā koutou, tēnā koutou, tēnā tātou katoa."

Following a smattering of cheers, and a loud "kia ora bro" from the cameraman for the indigenous Terra Ludus broadcasting corporation, Imelda then fronted for NBB, announcing that they would continue to pay Danny's salary and cover all her medical costs including nursing care, flights and travel for family support. She reiterated Manu's message that the best way to help Danny was to show support for her cause, the WWLB, and Simeon's that the family needed a stress-free environment in which to help Danny recover.

Simultaneously, in Santa Monica, ambulance and medical staff entered the alleyway behind Danny's apartment complex, quietly closed off by police who commandeered a residents' garden hose to create the illusion there was a water leak. Unimpeded, medical staff managed the delicate process of maneuvering Danny up the apartment's stairs and into her apartment on the second storey. By the time the media realized what was happening, through accessing images posted by residents of the tower overlooking the two-storey apartment complex, she was inside and hidden from public view. And she would remain so because, under the guise of renovations to assist Danny's recovery, NBB had also quietly invested in exterior paint and window coatings that blocked infrared and long-distance digital images, and disrupted drone or other forms of audio data collection. Simeon's company won the contract to ensure that no electronic communication in or out could be hacked.

Her mother and Auntie Marama moved into her apartment, leaving Danny's father to work the farm by himself. The spare bedroom, the larger of the two, was turned into marae-style sleeping, the floor complete with Danny's king-size futon and a single mattress to accommodate whoever was staying over. A nurse visited daily, to deal with Danny's feeding and evacuation tubes, and check on her condition. One of Danny's friends, an experienced neuro-physiotherapist who lived in the same complex, also visited daily to provide massage and physical exercises to maintain as much muscle tone as possible, and taught Danny's Mom additional exercises to keep Danny's body in shape. Throughout, Danny remained unresponsive. Not a twitch of a finger or change in expression indicated her inner state.

After two weeks, Simeon brought Bumbles back. "It might help her wake up," he said, backing through the front door with the cat carrier, disguised inside a large cardboard box in case of prying eyes. Bumbles immediately began meowing, scratching at the carrier door for release. Once free, he headed straight for the kitchen, and sat staring pointedly at the space where his food and water bowls should be.

"Hold your horses," Simeon said. "Give me a minute." Once the food and water were down, Bumbles' tail settled on the floor. Then he headed to Danny's bedroom. The shocked reaction was almost comic. Bumbles' back arched up, his tail bushed out, and he stood frozen in mid-stride when he saw the raised hospital bed in the place of Danny's floor-level futon.

Simeon quietly made his way to the elevated single bed and crouched down. "C'mon Bumbles. It's OK. Danny's here. Come and see." He stretched his hand towards the cat, index finger forward. Mistrustful, Bumbles slunk towards him. Simeon picked him up carefully (he'd had enough experience with those sharp claws) and placed him on the bed next to Danny. Bumbles sniffed Danny's hand and backed away, hackles up. Then he leapt off the bed and disappeared into the living room.

"Is he OK?" Simeon called.

"Under the couch," Danny's mother responded. "Safe enough for now. What happened?"

"He sniffed her hand then ran away." Simeon was confused. He knew how much that cat loved her. So he bent down and replicated the cat's actions. Ugh. Disinfectanty, hospitally, sickly. No wonder. It didn't smell like her at all. She was being cared for as a patient, not a person.

He headed for the bathroom, found a daily moisturizer, something with a graphic of a woman in a white plastic bottle, and a bottle of perfume. A wave of familiarity enveloped him as he did a test squirt, releasing a waft of citrus and soap. In her bedroom, he gently rubbed moisturizer into her hands and forearms, then tentatively on her face. A squirt of perfume here, and here, on the key pulse points at her wrists and neck. He slid into the chair beside the bed. Placed her hand in his. Laid his face on the pillow beside her head. Inhaled. Closed his eyes. Fought back tears. He'd bring Bumbles back later once the scents had settled. Danny needed that cat, and the cat needed her. Maybe, just maybe, it would make a difference.

Simeon kept working, spending evenings at the flat talking to Danny, keeping her up to date with the events of the league. He often stayed over Friday and Saturday nights, sleeping on the window seat, to give Danny's mother and any of the visiting Aunties a break. Maintaining a positive public face, even when blogging or talking to the media, was increasingly a challenge. But Friday nights were his. Just him and Bumbles and Danny. How it could have been. How it should have been.

One night, as hope slowly leached away, he turned her onto her side and carefully slid onto the bed to hold her, his arm tucked around her slender frame, even though he could hardly bear the reality of her strong muscles wasting away.

He wanted to talk to her, as he usually did, but words just wouldn't come. He was consumed by pain and fear and anger. So much anger at her for leaving him alone just when something had been flowering between them, fear that she wouldn't wake up or wouldn't remember him, or would be so changed that he wouldn't recognize her.

"This woman I love," he whispered to the back of her neck. "This woman. I love." He tasted the words, felt their weight, their truth, as each word shaped itself in his mouth. His frown slowly eased as their bodies shared warmth. This woman I love. The words reverberated in his head. All he could hear. And something more. He needed to move, to stand up.

So he untangled himself carefully and stood beside the bed, still holding her hand. "This woman I love." He said it louder, feeling an insane urge to dance. Said it again. Louder. Who the hell was here to hear anyway, except the cat? He began to turn slowly, arms spread wide, in the lonely room dominated by that institutional single bed. Repeating the words, as a bubble of laughter escaped, unexpected joy breaking through. Chanting and twirling, faster and faster. "This woman I love. I love. I love. I love. I love. Love. Love. Love. Love. Love." As the twirling slowly wound down, he folded into the bedside chair.

"She's not really here, but she's in here," he said to Bumbles who was watching him closely. "She's in here," deliberately thumping his closed fist against his heart. "Even if she never wakes up, even if she's not the same, she'll always be here."

Because Simeon refused to leave her side, the guys came to him. Saturdays were sacrosanct. Basketball days. Longer than before because the women's league started earlier. Eleventh hour for the first game, thirteenth hour for game two and fifteenth hour for game three, overlapping with early men's matches. Increasingly, they came together for the Sunday games as well, shifting their pick up games to mid-week evenings.

They set up the TV so he could see it from Danny's room, standing in the doorway. He made them play it loud enough so she could hear it too. The doctors said that people in comas could hear things so maybe this would help.

In the first month, he'd spent hours telling her all about the league, with special focus on Canestri Mulier. He read her the newspaper reports, his reviews of every game, discussed the line-ups, played her the Int-TV interviews and newscasts. He posted regularly to the website she had championed before the attack, including updates on her condition (nothing changed) and his weekly review of all the matches. Much to his surprise, he built up a following and he told her about that as well. Read her the drafts of his posts. Laughed and read her the responses of fans to his take on the state of play.

He tried not to doubt. She could hear him. She was interested.

COMING BACK

She regained consciousness as the regular season entered its last three weeks. The guys were in the living room yelling at Canestri Mulier who were 10 points down heading towards half-time. The smell of popcorn was in the air and they were getting louder with each beer. He heard a rustle and a croak that sounded something like "CM?" His heart skipped a beat, nearly stopped completely. He didn't want to look, didn't think he could bear it if he'd imagined it. The others were all focused on the screen. He turned slowly, unconsciously praying to Gaia or perhaps to the universe itself. Her eyes were mere slits, but open.

He tried to act normally. "CM?" he repeated, his voice cracking.

An almost imperceptible nod, as if she couldn't remember what to do. He felt the same, like his brain was wading through mud. "They're down 10 points, nearly half time. Canestri Illicium are shooting the lights out from the 3-point line and they can't stop them."

Her eyes closed and he panicked. He grabbed her hand. "Squeeze if you can still hear me." A slight movement. "Is it too loud?" He was sure he detected a slight head shake. "I'll be back in a sec, OK?" Squeeze. "Stay right there. Don't go away."

Prig. The nurse wouldn't be back until tomorrow. What should he do? Ring the hospital? Ring the doctor? Ring her parents? Yes. Tell the guys? No. No. Definitely not. They'd been drinking for three hours. They'd be sure to do something wrong. They were too loud. They'd just freak her out. But all he wanted to do was run around the apartment yelling, "she's awake, she's awake".

He could hear them grumping about the game. "We gotta do something," Mike said. "Those prigging Muliers are throwing the game away. Danny would never put up with that. Let's vid the damn

coach, that prigging Denise, and remind her who they're playing for."
Mike had Simeon's icom in his hand, scrolling through his contacts.
Then, like a lightning bolt, the answer thrummed through Simeon.

"Give it to me," he demanded. His tone and expression must
have been enough because Mike handed it over without arguing.
"Tell me what happens at half time," he directed, retreating into the
bedroom. "But I was gonna tell that coach…" Mike started. "I'll do
it," Simeon growled. "You just stay on top of what's happening."

He inserted his earplugs and Denise's stern face appeared
immediately. "Yes. Is this urgent? We're in the middle of a game." He
could understand her shortness.

"It's Simeon," he said. "I've got some news but you've got to
keep it quiet."

"What is it? Half-time's almost over."

"Danny just woke up," he said, amazed to find himself saying
the words.

"What?" Denise's voice screamed across the airwaves, nearly
bursting his eardrums before the auto-adjust kicked in. "For real?"

"Yes. For real. And her first words were CM. So you really,
really, need to win this game. I think following you is what brought
her back, at least briefly. So can you tell the girls and please win this
one game."

"Look Sim, I've got to go but I'll tell them. It's exactly the
motivation they need."

"Remember it has to stay a secret though. I haven't even had
time to tell her parents and we don't know how permanent it is."

"You got it," and the link was severed.

Simeon speed-vidded her parents. "You need to come home
now," he started. "Danny just woke up." He rushed on, not wanting
to raise their hopes too high. "She just spoke a couple of words and
went back to sleep but she's conscious and she knows what's going on.
Come home now. Please." He couldn't bear it alone.

"Be there in an hour," her dad said and sliced out.

A yell from the living room signaled the start of the second
half.

Simeon couldn't be still. He paced. He watched the game for five seconds, returned to Danny's bedside, held her hand, checked her breathing, whispered in her ear, "wake up." Went back to the door. Back to the bed. Like being stoned, or on speed, or something. He didn't know. He wanted to laugh, to yell, to sprint, to just do something. In the end he couldn't help himself. He marched into the living room, and planted himself in front of the screen, ignoring the guys' yells of protest to get out of the way.

"Shut up," he said. "Danny's awake. She woke up." The boys went silent, only the now overloud commentary, music and crowd cheers reverberating in the room.

"Audio off," Simeon demanded and silence descended. "But she's gone back under. She hasn't stirred for 10 minutes. I don't know what to do."

Mike was the first to react. "Sit. Listen to the game," he ordered, vacating the best seat and steering a passive Simeon over to it. "This is why she woke up, right? Because of the game. You need to be able to tell her what happened." Mike handed him a beer from the cooler. "Drink. You need it." Then, pointing at Dominic, he said, "You watch Danny for the next 15 minutes. And be quiet. Don't crowd her. Then Con, then me." He turned back to Simeon. "Who've you told?"

"Her Mom and Dad. They're on their way here. And Denise. She's told the team I think."

"That's why they're doing so well then." Turning to the screen, Mike demanded "Audio on" and the sound returned. "Watch. They're up by 15 points. They came out of half-time on fire. We couldn't figure out why. What about Auntie Marama, Manu?"

"No."

"OK. I'll call them. You watch the game."

And that's how it went for the next 30 minutes. Canestri Mulier dominant. Simeon in shock. The guys taking turns watching over Danny. The game ended with CM the winners, now leading the league. In the post-match interview, Denise dedicated the win to Danny. The team stood behind her in a semi-circle. When Denise said, "This win's for Daniela Bartoli and so will the next one be," the players linked hands and raised them above their heads.

"For Danny," they chanted as one. It was a powerful image, like the silent candle vigils outside the hospital in the early days after the shooting. Only this time it was 15 sweaty women. Spontaneously, the stadium crowd took up the gesture. The cameras swept the stadium interior as group after group of fans linked arms and silently raised them. Danny's parents burst through the door as the post-game celebration was in full swing on court.

"They won?" Her dad waited for the answer before disappearing into Danny's room. Her mother was already there. Simeon still sat, eyes closed, hearing only the sounds. A shake of the arm brought him back. "Snap out of it," Mike demanded. "Get in there."

"They're her parents," he responded. "They deserve time alone with her."

"Sure. But you're the one who was there when she woke up. They need to talk to you. But they can't do that with all of us out here. So you go in there. And we'll clean up and get out of here."

Mike had to haul him up to his feet. He turned Simeon towards the bedroom and gave him a push. Turning to the others, Mike said, "C'mon guys. Pick everything up. We'll hit Maxine's BBQ. They'll have the rest of the basketball on."

RECOVERY?

By the time the nurse arrived on Sunday at eighth hour, Danny was awake again. Simeon and Danny's parents had each shared part of the night at Danny's beside, talking to each other or to her. They knew she could hear even if she couldn't respond.

After he explained what he'd seen and heard, he gave them the first shift. She was their daughter, he was just the … the what? He could hardly call himself her boyfriend since they'd never even been on an official date. Friend was insufficient. Her parents accepted his being there and had authorized him to talk to the media. They'd known him for five years and never questioned him.

He passed out of conscious knowing within minutes of stretching out on the couch. His last coherent thought was that he was pleased the boys had cleaned up. He woke to a reverberating purr underlain by the murmur of a voice in the next room. Bumbles was on his chest, kneading purposively and firmly. Hard to sleep through that. He knew not to move quickly. That would lead to pain and he hadn't mastered the art of clipping Bumbles' claws, so they were sharper than usual. Indicating by small movements his intention to sit up, Bumbles grumpily gave way. Simeon swung his feet to the floor and rose, moving the blanket-wrapped cat to a secure position on the couch. As he walked towards Danny's room he caught the conversation and stopped.

"…don't know what your relationship was before, but it's clear he's in love with you. And we approve." It was Danny's Mom speaking. "You should see the way he takes care of that damn cat. It follows him round like a dog. And we know Bumbles is a good judge of character. So keep this in mind when you come back to us. Even if you can't remember everything, know this. That young man is a keeper. Dad's asleep now and I'm going to join him. You need a bit of quiet time I think. But we're all here waiting. OK?"

By the time she finished, Simeon had stepped quietly backwards until he reached the open doorway into the kitchen and was plugging in the kettle, and starting to unload the dishdrawer. He acted surprised when she appeared at the doorway.

"Morning," she said. "Or almost. I'm heading to bed. Do you want to keep an eye on Danny?"

"Sure. I've just woken up thanks to Bumbles. He seems to think fifth hour is an excellent time for breakfast. Would you like a cup of chai?"

"No thanks. It's been a long night. But a good one wouldn't you say? It's not every day your daughter comes back to you."

Or the love of your life, he wanted to say, but didn't. "I'm sorry you weren't here," he said instead. "It's hopeful isn't it? That she'll come back for sure. She knew what was happening, so that's a good sign isn't it?"

"Yes it is," patting him on the shoulder. "Now you go and sit with her. Her dad and I have been talking to her all night, so if you just want to sit, that would be fine."

It sounded a little like a recommendation and he was happy with that. He appreciated that they were willing to share her with him in this way. He sat beside her. Then carefully shifted to the narrow mattress to spoon with her. Her parents would be asleep for a while and he needed the comfort. Only for a few minutes. He dreamed she was holding his hand, murmuring his name. But it wasn't like his usual dreams. Her voice was rusty, croaky. And it was this that brought him back to full awareness. Her voice. And her hand actually holding his.

"Sim. You?"

"Yes. It's me. I'm sorry. Do you want me to move? Sorry for this. I didn't ask your permission. Sorry." He was babbling. Had never thought of how she might feel to wake and find a man wrapped around her.

"Stop," she whispered. Exerting a little bit of grasp as he tried to move his arm from around her waist. "Stay."

"I need to tell your parents," he said. "They're here. Sleeping."

"Know," she rasped. "Stay." And he did, wrapped around her, sharing warmth. Neither of them saying anything. When her hand released his, he knew she was either asleep or gone again. He untangled himself, careful not to snag the intravenous feeding line. Moved to the chair, keeping one hand in his. He wanted to her to know, no matter where she was that he was with her.

When her parents returned three hours later, she was fully awake. Eyes open, watching over Simeon who, even in sleep, held her right hand in his. She shook her head at them, managed a tiny smile and a silent kiss.

"Chai?" her Dad mouthed. She nodded. Her Mom quietly came to the other side of the bed.

"Better wake him," she whispered before kissing Danny on the forehead and leaving the room.

Danny squeezed Simeon's hand. He woke instantly, and she saw how attuned to her movements he was. He opened his eyes and, in that unguarded moment, revealed it all to her. Then he closed them, released her hand. "Hi," he said. "You're back."

"So seem," she replied. "Back. Where? Why bed?

"You don't remember?" Shock was evident on his features. Then he composed himself. "Let's wait 'til your Mom and Dad wake up. Then we can talk. You don't feel sleepy?"

A single, slow shake of the head indicated no. Then he heard the clatter of cups and the fridge opening. "I'll be back in a minute," he said. "OK?"

A slow nod was accompanied by a tiny lip twitch, the beginnings of a smile he hoped.

In the kitchen, both faces turned toward him. "She's awake. Really awake. You need to see her. Talk to her. I'll finish the tea."

Neither said a word, just walked out. He noticed there were four cups, not the usual three. Two chai, two coffee. Did they know? Or were they being optimistic? Doesn't matter, he decided. She's awake and she loves chai, so that's what she's getting.

He consciously moved slowly. Not wanting to intrude, and beginning to mull over her first responses. But when the drinks started to cool a little, he added eggnog to one chai, loaded the tray and brought all four cups into the room. The tableaux stopped him at the doorway. One parent either side, each with a hand in their own. Danny slowly switching her focus from side to side. She turned a questioning gaze on him.

"Real?"

"Real," he replied. "All true." He didn't know what they'd said but he thought she wouldn't be able to cope with too much complexity to begin with. Whatever had been said, he was agreeing with it.

"Chai?" was the next question.

"With eggnog," he agreed, unconsciously curling his upper lip. It was such a bizarre combination of flavors. He had never understood her attraction to it. "You want it?"

She nodded. So he handed it to her mother, who tested the temperature and brought it slowly to Danny's lips. None of them was sure whether this was allowed. She still had the feeding and evacuation systems attached. Danny inhaled, sheer pleasure crossing her features.

"Just a tiny sip," her mother advised. "We're not sure if you can drink anything or not." Danny's tongue stretched towards the liquid. Touched the surface. Tasted. Disappeared back into her mouth. She repeated the action. Smiled and laid her head back on the pillow, eyes closing. "Bumbles?"

"On the couch, in a blanket," Simeon replied. "He'd be happy to finish it."

"Finish what?" Her father asked his first question.

"The chai," replied Simeon. "He gets a chai eggnog in his bowl once a week. Don't ask me why he likes it. That cat is very odd."

"Always. Likes." Danny's whisper.

Simeon explained. "Danny always saves a little bit in the bottom of her cup for him. So I give him some every Saturday night." He realized he had already shifted to present tense in relation to Danny. A good sign, surely.

"A chai-eggnog-drinking cat. That's one for the books," her Dad replied. "Go on then."

IT'S ALL ALRIGHT

Danny spent two weeks back in hospital – for assessment they said, but her parents had seen enough on Terra Ludus to know it was as much celebrity-watching on the part of doctors and nursing staff. They needed to assess her cognitive responses, ease her medication, assist her with re-learning how to walk and balance, and for transitioning from an intravenous liquid diet. It would be several weeks at least before she should consume much fiber or eat more than tiny meals. And, as the days passed, it became clear that it might be some time before she could talk normally. NBB employed a speech therapist, who worked with Danny daily. She understood everything and her responses were appropriate but her speech centers were still jumbled. She had trouble with many verbs and all pronouns. And she only had one tense – the present. Her sentences were truncated, simple but at least on the right track.

Danny, her parents and Simeon met with Imelda and Arjun who talked them into an initial interview with NBB, to be aired as post-season began, promoted via photographs only. Danny agreed only if Emilie was her stylist, and chose the hairdresser and outfit. Her other condition was that the interview be as short as possible. She was slow and weak, physically and mentally, and could only tolerate limited periods of interaction before falling asleep. Arjun left a single sheet of five questions for her to consider. The interview would be filmed on a Tuesday, three days before airing, and Danny and her parents would have some veto over what could be broadcast.

Emilie's visit brought normality slightly closer, even though she struggled to contain her shock at Danny's condition. "Bonjour, skinny girl," Emilie tried to joke, "what are we going to do with you?" She turned her professional gaze over the wasted body, jutting cheekbones, dry skin and limp hair. Then she reached over and gave Danny a hug. Just held her, softly. "You tell me what you're capable of, mon amie, and I'll work with that," she whispered. "You're the driver, I'm the navigator. D'accord?" She drew back but they held hands still. "What look do you want to go for? There are two main options. We can play up the change, the effect of the attack, emphasize the sympathy angle, or we can try to disguise it, get as close to what you looked like before, emphasize the 'old you' coming back as strong as ever."

"What think?" pointing at Emilie. "Trust judgment." Then shook her head no as she said, "Not pity." She was sure of that. "What," pointing to herself, "look like before?"

Emilie gave it to her straight. "Cheek implants, probably. Fake tan, haircut and dye, some clever layering of clothes. You'll be shot in bed." Emilie's eyes widened as a look of horror crossed her face. "Merde! Sorry. I mean you'll be dressed in the hospital bed for the photo."

Danny laughed aloud for the first time, the husky sound surprising both of them. "Not sorry. Not worry. Really. Not remember. Start run and…" she shrugged her shoulders, indicating 'I don't know'. "See daytime, say dark. Now …" she paused rummaging through her mind for the word. Began again, forcing the verb to exit. "Now think what look like 'dress in hospital bed'. Not sure Vogue." She waved towards herself and the bed, smiling "All wear for months."

Emilie's shoulders relaxed and she launched a genuine grin in Danny's direction. "Très drôle. Haven't lost your sense of humor I see." She gave Danny's hand a squeeze before continuing. "The problem is that some of those things won't really work in a live interview. The collagen implants will hinder your speech. You'll feel and sound strange. Probably not the impression you want. Most people take some time to adjust. And we don't have that amount of time."

Danny looked at her steadily.

"So I'd rather work with what we have. Stay away from the high fashion anorexia look – although you could certainly pull that off right now. Try to reconstruct a natural look somehow. And it's still officially winter here so you can wear long sleeves." She was tapping the end of an eye pencil against her teeth, thinking, weighing up possibilities, options.

All Danny could think was that Emilie had used the word natural without sarcasm.

"Sure alright?" indicating towards Emilie.

"Yes." Surprised. "Why?"

"Know you months? Never..." she mimed speaking, then dredged up the verb. "Never say 'natural'. Not good. World on head? You wrong? Me wrong?"

Emilie hooted. "Incroyable. You're truly amazing. You haven't lost your wits. That's a relief."

Pointing again at Emilie, Danny managed, "not blonde dolly." Danny was enjoying herself except for the frustration of flubbing her lines. Her mind was fine but it felt like a drunken waiter was carrying her words from mind to mouth. Still, Emilie seemed to get it, and she was feeling better with each bit of banter.

"Je comprends. Oui. Well you were – and still are – one of a kind. No blonde dolly. Which ..." she paused, tapping her eye pencil again, "makes me think that's the way to go. You didn't look like anyone else. And you still don't. Just in a more extreme way. I've got it. Leave it to me. Can I bring the hairdresser later this week? Same time?"

Danny shrugged her assent, now leaning back, eyes closed, feeling the wave of tiredness sweeping over her. The last thing she remembered was Emilie muttering, "I wonder if I can bring the hair colorist in as well. Better ask the nurses."

When she woke it was dark. The door was closed and the room illuminated only by the dull orange glow of streetlights. Someone was holding her hand. Simeon. She could tell by the way her closed fist fit snugly into his palm, by the smoothness of his skin. By his scent. By the particular quality of his stillness. He was tired, emanating little outward energy. She savored the moment. Not sure what she would say to him. As soon as she moved, rolling towards him, he was alert. Leaning forward, his face initially inches from hers. As he started to pull back, letting her hand go, she reached towards him, encouraging him closer. Unbidden, the memory of pulling Adie's head towards her for the SportsLive kiss appeared. She couldn't help it. She started giggling. Simeon started to pull away again. This time she exerted more pressure.

"Don't," she said. "Not laugh you. Like kiss Adie. Not want. First kiss we." She watched his pupils widen, his nostrils flare, the sudden flush in his cheeks. "Is first kiss?"

He flushed even more visibly.

"Is?" She was still half smiling. "Take advantage, Sleeping Princess?"

"No. No. No." He pulled out of her hands, shaking his head as if trying to dislodge a vision. He was bright red. "No. I…" He was bereft of words.

"Come. Here," she said. "What do, know help. Know Sim," tapping his chest. "Know you. Coma. Learn more." Now he was flushing in waves, eyes wide. Facial muscles frozen.

She began to worry about what had him so freaked out. It couldn't be that bad. Could it? A frisson of doubt crept in at his silence, his rigidity.

"What do you remember?"

She shrugged to indicate not much. "Words. Phrases. Sense. Feel. Always know." She took his hand in hers. "Know you. Not wrong feel. Not wrong sense. Warm." She squeezed his hand. "Feel more." Her own cheeks began to flame and simultaneously she frowned, unable to convey her meaning, sure she was not making sense. "Please. Here. Talk. Kiss." She wasn't sure about saying the last part aloud but it was what she wanted. Something tender and soft.

But it wasn't like that at all. Chair shoved aside, Sim was kneeling at her side in an instant. Strong hands gripping both sides of her face. His mouth strong and warm and demanding. Hovering between asking and taking. And then they were both over the edge. She could taste it, as heady as Terra Sparta dessert wine, smooth and rich, intoxicating. Then there was no thinking at all, until a rather loud knock on the glass wall disrupted them.

Sim reluctantly released her, looking as flushed and shocked as she imagined she did. They both turned to the window.

Dad, thought Danny, *what awful timing*. Prig, thought Simeon, now I'm in trouble. Dad waved and pointed down the hall. I'll get a coffee, he mimed, leaving them alone.

Simeon took a deep breath. Life was too short to be held back by doubts. He knelt on the floor beside her bed. "I love you," he said. "I was already in love with you before the incident. I will always love you. And if you don't love me, or don't think there's a chance you could, can you please tell me. Because I can't live anywhere near you if I'm not with you."

He looked tragic, she thought. Brave and afraid in equal measure. How could she not love him? She knew she'd fallen in love before the shooting – *why does everyone keep calling it the incident? Shut up random thought*. He loved her, he loved her cat, and he showed it in everything he had done for her.

She didn't say anything. Just leaned down and kissed him. Gently this time. A single kiss. A promise. And leaned back. The joy stealing across his face was like a sunrise.

"Really?"

"Really."

"You're sure?"

"Sure as woman," pointing to her head, "with brain injury."

He was still down on his knees.

"In that case, Daniela Bartoli, will you take me, Simeon Autlander, to be your life partner, to have and hold, through sickness and in health, in richness and poverty, for as long as we both shall live?" The proposal, unexpected as it was, was completely Simeon. Serious but self-mocking at the same time. Confident and hesitant. Giving her an out, if she needed one.

She took her time, needing every ounce of concentration to get this right. She placed her other hand over his and, pointing to herself, intoned, "Me, unsound body mind, yes take partner, have, hold, sick, health, rich (pointing at him), poor (pointing at herself) for life. Yes idiot (pointing at him again). Yes partner." In lieu of saying you (a word she still couldn't force into voice), she kissed him again. Fast, hard, quick. "Today. Tomorrow. Ever." She wanted to joke and in her

217

mind she said, *You better do it before I regain my mental faculties.*" But all she could extrude into the world was "before normal."

The next thing she knew she was out of bed, swung into his arms as he headed for the corridor – pausing to check her legs wouldn't hit the door frame on the way out – and her parents. He stopped five feet away from them, not sure what to say. So Danny said it for him.

"We partner. No wait. Fast?" Dad strode towards them, clasping them both in a bear hug. "Fantastic," he said, squeezing them hard. "Couldn't have asked for anything more. My daughter back and a decent choice for a partner-son. The world moves in mysterious ways."

Mom was trying to squeeze in. On tiptoes, she kissed Simeon's cheek and patted it. Side on, she pressed her forehead against Danny's, looking deep into her eyes. Then nodded. Danny started to feel claustrophobic.

"Aaah," she half-moaned, knowing they'd listen. "Room?" Her parents backed off like startled rabbits. "Sim. Down. Stand." And he returned her to the floor holding her upright. And her parents rejoined them. A standing circle of four.

Then they heard the clapping. From the doctors and nurses at the medical station, visible 10 feet down the corridor. They progressed towards them, Danny wobbling, supported by Simeon on one side, her Dad on the other. But walking. Towards happiness. Towards normality. Towards those who had the power to release her back to the real world, something she wanted as fast as possible.

THE FINAL

As part of her recovery, she agreed to a second interview, to be aired during the best-of-three finals series. She convinced NBB to let Simeon come on set. "Micro-celeb," she said. "Autlandish blog. News/gossip crossover. 'Shoot victim find life partner, CM finals old team.' Got everything. Can help," pointing to herself, "walk on set. Not wheelchair. Not pity."

After NBB offered to fly Auntie Marama and Manu over for third game if the series went that far, she also agreed to host an NBB camera during the final game. They scheduled the interview for after the Saturday news hour, on the sports show, just like her first interview. The only difference was that they filmed it on Thursday. It would appear plausibly live and the final would broadcast live an hour later. She slept 20 hours on Friday. She wanted to be awake to see the interview and the whole game. They were going to Mike's. Her parents, Manu and Auntie Marama, Emilie, the guys of course, and even Nancy and Vic. NBB sent one cam-op for live reactions during the match. Mike was ecstatic. His status in the quiz night crowd would go stratospheric.

What none of them knew was that NBB had also stationed a camera in Altrix Prison with the shooter. They showed him during the pre-game. The sound was down as usual, barely audible as various people ferried food and beer, found their seats, chatted about the match to come. A gasp of horror swept the room when Hillman Dale's face appeared on screen. Danny was surprised, wondering who it was to cause such a reaction. A prisoner clearly, in the full-body pink jumpsuit. A hint of dark facial growth, a pleasant face, innocuous.

Mike almost exploded out of his chair, his beer raised as if he wanted to throw it through the screen, shouting, "What the prig?

Prigging NBB. What the prigging prig do they think they're doing?" Striding towards the camera operator, he upbraided him: "What the hell is going on? Turn off the camera. Now."

Danny saw the red light go out and she kept an eye on it. Whatever was happening, she didn't want it recorded.

"Are you OK dear?" Dad was on one knee in front of her, his weather-beaten face creased with worry.

"Fine," she said. "Who that? Why upset?"

"She doesn't know," Nancy's voice was almost breathless.

"You don't know?" Constantin's disbelief was evident in his slightly hysterical rising vocalization.

"Know what?"

Sim was now beside her. "That's the shooter," he said. "The guy who put you in the hospital, who killed Kiwane. NBB, those prigging bastards, must have decided to boost ratings by showing you and him during the game. What the prig were they thinking?"

He leapt up. "I'm vidding that prigging Arjun right now." And he disappeared into the kitchen, pulling, almost slamming, the sliding door closed. Under, and sometimes over, the babble in the living room, all she could hear were longish periods of silence, punctuated by Simeon's short, increasingly loud but still indecipherable responses. The face was now gone, the images showing the studio hosts, and graphics of the teams, athletes, positions. All the usual stuff. Her brain hurt. *That was the guy? The scary shooter? But he looked so normal. It doesn't make any sense.*

"Look," she finally said. "It alright. See face, mean nothing," pointing to the screen where it originally appeared. "Tell Sim. Not worry. Please."

As Mike slid open the kitchen door, she caught a glimpse of Simeon's face reddened with anger. He was rhythmically banging his head against a cupboard above the bench, the icom in danger of dropping from his right hand. Mike reached towards it, simultaneously sliding the door shut.

"Volume up," Danny demanded of the screen. She raised her voice as it responded. "NBB not matter. CM final. Prime time. Kick Illicium ass. Yes?

Called by the audio, Mike and Sim returned, Mike's arm loosely slung across Simeon's shoulders. Danny patted the spot on the couch beside her. "Here," she said. "Sit." She grasped his hand, squeezed hard. "OK. Not hurt. Not remember. Nothing." She bent her head to his. "Let go. Here for fun. Like old times. CM play final!" Then she whispered. "Boys watch. World on head, right?"

A glimmer of a smile and the slight loss of tension in his shoulders were good signs, as he replied. "You're right. Let's not spoil it for them. After this season, they'll never be able to say women can't play."

It felt like only minutes before the half-time whistle blew. It was a tight, physical contest. There were no obvious injuries but more than a few bodies hit the floor. Canestri Mulier had the slight edge, consistently holding a 2 to 10 point lead.

The commentators were giving viewing stats. NBB's full immersion package had completely sold out, billions of viewers world-wide were tuned in, and even the advance Mars team were getting the game relayed. NBB had a camera there as well. *Bizarre. Women's ball beamed into space?* NBB were giving this final everything they had. *And more power to them,* Danny thought. *I wouldn't have sunk so low as to exploit human suffering for ratings, but that's the way things work. Doesn't mean I have to be part of it.*

Somehow, when the studio commentators threw to Mike's living room, she wasn't surprised, even though they'd been given no prior warning. She'd seen the cameraman hoist his camera at the end of the half and the red light come on, so she was prepared. In studio, the hosts were setting it up. "So, we have a camera with Daniela Bartoli as well today, the woman whose vid started this whole extravaganza, and who has recently emerged from a coma after being shot by a disgruntled men's basketball fan. Daniela, what did you think of the first half?"

She looked the camera lens in the eye. "Fantastic. Best ever. CM", she waved her hands to cover her loss of the verb, "awesome. Not biased." She tried to smile broadly, sharing the joke with whoever was watching.

"What about Canestri Illicium? What do you make of their play?" the host returned, obviously primed to ask easy questions.

"Good fight. Good coach. Wish both luck." She combined a shrug and a smile to indicate her enjoyment, before ending with "heart with CM."

"And you have probably seen that we have a camera in Terra Ludus Prison with the man who shot you. What do you have to say to him, as this now incredibly successful and popular league comes to its conclusion?"

She knew it. She'd known it from the moment she understood who the man was. But she wasn't playing their game anymore.

"Hope enjoy game," she said. "Tell me," waving towards the others in the room, "basketball fan. This best ever. Top class. Love basketball, love this."

The commentator paused, seemingly not quite sure where to go next. It would appear she wasn't playing to their expected script.

"So, what would you say to him about what he did to you and to Kiwane Shallcrass, the two people whose lives he has forever changed?"

"More than two," she responded. "Send care Kiwane family, friends. Great athlete, great ref, good person, support women's game. Know watch tonight. Loss to all basketball. Not bad feeling to shooter."

As the words left her mouth, she realized it was true. She took a few seconds to frame a complete sentence with all the right parts.

"He lives with this. Help me see life is precious, live every moment. What I do." She leaned in towards Simeon's shoulder, resting her head on it, making the camera include him in shot, gathering strength for one last statement.

"Wish him same." Then she sat upright again, Simeon's arm now curved around her shoulders.

The commentators were silent. As was Mike's living room. They were all staring at her. But she knew not to take her gaze away from the camera.

"Well. That's very interesting. Thank you Daniela Bartoli for your thoughts." As the red light went out, she slumped, almost collapsed, as if whatever string had been holding her upright had suddenly been severed. The commentators continued their predetermined show. As she anticipated, they went straight to the prison. As Hillman Dale came on screen she closed her eyes.

"Volume off," she murmured. Nothing happened until Manu repeated it for her, much louder. "Volume off. Screen blank. 5 minutes." She didn't care what Dale had to say. It was his life and he had to deal with it.

Vic was kneeling behind the couch stroking her hair. "You did good," she whispered. "It's always better to forgive. Then you can move on. I'm proud of you." Soothing with her hands and voice, "You can let go now. It's done. It's over."

The others stared at her, their gazes burning like laser beams. Auntie Marama and Mom stood like statues, hand-in-hand, drawing strength from each other. Dad was face-to-face with the camera guy, urgency in his stance, so close the blast of air from his anger ruffled the guy's hair.

"Get out now," he demanded. "NBB's had its pound of flesh, its sound bite. It's bad enough that the guy shot her, but now you want to exploit her pain and put her through more suffering? It's enough. You're not welcome here. If you don't leave, I'll call the peacekeepers." He had his hand on the guy's back. Manu moved to stand beside him. Yet, far from resisting, the cameraman was moving rapidly, almost fleeing. The front door slammed.

And it was then that she realized she would never be going back to NBB. The league was launched, the world was watching and she would probably slide back into anonymity. She was a bit-player in a bigger game and her part was done. She'd rehab her way to fitness, go back to freelancing, help Simeon with the blog, or keep developing her own vlog. Perhaps she could score some paid work as a travel writer, given her vlog's success. But a quieter life beckoned. She'd be a supporter in the background. Out of the spotlight. Well away from threats and abuse and danger. *And make up and fashion.* She smiled to herself – the thought of a return to late rising and spending the day in her pjs or track pants very appealing. It was hard to believe that it was those connections to fashion and travel that had underpinned the league's success. *And human drama I guess. Why else would they have a camera here and in the prison?*

She gathered her remaining energy and leaned forward, wanting to enjoy. It didn't matter how it had happened, only that it had. Let NBB do what they would. Right now she was here for the basketball, for the women who had worked so hard and for so long for this recognition and respect.

"Look," she said. "All that," she waved her hand dismissing it, "not matter. On NBB. Not me, not you. More important. There." She pointed to the screen, which had returned showing images but no sound. "Basketball. What here for. What matters. Right now. Stop look like fall over in shock. Not chance. Relax. Enjoy. Cheer loud. Best team win."

"Yeah," Mike pumped his fist. "You're right. And we know which team it ought to be. Audio up."

As their faces rotated back towards the screen, like flowers to the sun, she slipped her hand into Simeon's, rested her head on his shoulder and crossed her fingers for the right outcome.

SUGGESTED CLASSROOM AND BOOK CLUB USE

DISCUSSION OR HOMEWORK QUESTIONS

1. *Terra Ludus* reveals the power of the cultural belief that it is primarily men's sport that is culturally important. Conduct a content analysis of sports news to see how much coverage is given to sportsmen and how much to sportswomen.

2. Public responses on news and online sites to Daniela's 'suggestion' that NBB provide more coverage of women's basketball reveal the realities of standing up against dominant ideologies. Conduct a thematic analysis and summarize the main themes in these responses. Compare these themes to a recent case where someone has been publicly attacked for their opinions, and identify the similarities and differences.

3. The expectations of how female bodies look and dress can be very different in sport and in media. Identify the moments when Daniela encounters these expectations and discuss how she navigates her way around them, explaining whether you think she is oriented more towards a sporting or a feminine form of embodiment.

4. Terra Ludus explores the strategies that women might use to carve out cultural, and actual, space in the public realm. Identify some of the actions taken by the main characters that disrupt existing ways of devaluing women. Identify the spheres of culture outside sport that NBB taps into in order to make the league successful.

5. Issues related to how far media corporations will go to attract viewers arise in several parts of the novel. From the perspective of media responsibility, discuss whether NBB was right to place cameras with Daniela and with Hillman Dale during the final game (Chapter 32).

6. In sport, female participants often have to counter expectations that they are weaker, slower and less competent than men. Provide examples from the novel of when Daniela encounters these expectations. How are these issues reflected in your own life? Give

225

examples from your own experiences of what Physical Education teachers, sports coaches or friends and family have said or done to support or challenge this belief.

7. *Terra Ludus* imagines a completely different future for professional sport. Discuss the advantages and disadvantages for media, professional sport and fans if all professional sport was located in one country. What would be gained or lost? Compare this vision to current discussions about the future of the Olympic Games, which range from locating it permanently in one place to holding different events in different countries over a longer period of time.

CREATIVE WRITING ASSIGNMENTS

1. Choose a minor character and create a back-story for that person.
2. Select any of the characters and fast-forward five years. Write a short story about where they are now.
3. Pick one scene and rewrite it from the perspective of another character.
4. Write an alternative ending to *Terra Ludus*.

PERFORMANCE ACTIVITIES

1. Select a scene and perform it, focusing on bringing the characters to life in terms of how they move, dress, and interact.

ABOUT THE AUTHOR

Toni Bruce, Ph.D., is a sport sociologist and media studies scholar based at the Faculty of Education and Social Work, University of Auckland, New Zealand. Her career has taken her around the world, from New Zealand to the UK, United States and Australia. She received her PhD in sociology of sport from the University of Illinois, Champaign-Urbana, USA. Originally trained as a news reporter, she has also worked in sports journalism and as a sports columnist. She has published more than 70 articles and book chapters in the areas of sport sociology and sports media, and co-edited two ground-breaking books on women's sport. *Sportswomen at the Olympics: A global content analysis of newspaper coverage* (2010, Sense Publishers, with Jorid Hovden & Pirkko Markula) was the largest international investigation of media coverage of women's sport, and brought together researchers from 18 countries and 14 different languages. *Outstanding: Research about Women and Sport in New Zealand* (2008, Wilf Malcolm Institute of Educational Research, with Camilla Obel & Shona Thompson) was the first major edited collection of research on the experiences of women in sport in New Zealand. She has recently delivered invited keynote speeches or symposia presentations in the USA, Japan, China, South Korea, Switzerland and France. Her strong belief in the role of the university as the critic and conscience of society means that she has made regular appearances as an expert on media representation and gender on radio in New Zealand, Australia and the USA. She has published more than 70 newspaper columns and articles on sports websites, and her recent research on rugby and nationalism received media attention in nine countries, including France, the UK and Chile. She irregularly reflects on the state of play in sport on her low-visibility blog at bigpicturesport.com

Printed in the United States
By Bookmasters